Clem Sunter

HOME TRUTHS

*What we've got
to* do!

TAFELBERG

HUMAN & ROUSSEAU

PREVIOUS BOOKS BY THE AUTHOR

The World and South Africa in the 1990s
South African Environments into the 21st Century
(with Brian Huntley and Roy Siegfried)
The New Century
Pretoria will Provide and Other Myths
The Casino Model
The High Road: Where are we now?
What it really takes to be World Class

First published in 1998 jointly by
Tafelberg Publishers Ltd, 28 Wale Street, Cape Town
and Human & Rousseau (Pty) Ltd,
State House, 3-9 Rose Street, Cape Town

Cover design and typography by Jürgen Fomm
Typeset in 10,5 on 13 pt Palatino and
printed and bound by National Book Printers,
Drukkery Street, Goodwood, Western Cape,
South Africa

First edition 1998
Second impression 1999
ISBN 0 624 03724 X

TO PAT, LINETTE,
JILL AND JÜRGEN

*For being simply the
best publishing team around*

CONTENTS

Economic Crossroads

We still have to discover the formula for economic success. Please hurry up! Facta non verba – *we need deeds, not words.*

10.11.1996 I would like to deal with the latest scenarios for South Africa.

Back in 1986 we stressed that the immediate future of the country centred on the political choices facing the National Party at the time. Either they could negotiate with the real leaders, in which case sanctions would be dropped, South Africa would re-enter the world arena and we would take the "High Road". Or they could co-opt a bunch of tame representatives into the Cabinet, in which case sanctions would remain, the masses would revolt and we would take the "Low Road".

A simple choice and the Nats made the right one. Now we face a second fork in the road ahead. It revolves around the economic choices available to the nation as a whole. Either the government and the private sector together spread the business ethic throughout the land and thereby create a new entrepreneurial class and we evolve into the first "African lion" in the early part of the next century. Or we experience a failure of economic growth, in which case we inevitably descend into a vicious circle of government crackdowns to stop anarchy, interspersed with periods of populism where impossible promises of redistribution of wealth are made to the masses and come to nothing.

We call this circle the "Argentinian tango" after the pattern that country went through following the Second World War, when it alternated between the generals and the Perons (Juan and Eva and then Isabel). Luckily, Argentina managed to escape the circle and is now considered one of the more successful nations in South America, having ditched the dirigisme and socialism of the 1970s for the free-market policies of today.

9

However, the more likely result for South Africa, if it tumbles around inside the circle, is the destruction of civil society and a growing internal conflict which spreads to the region as a whole. The outcome is a highly polarised and criminalised society. South Africa turns into an impoverished wasteland. Effectively, it ceases to exist when it fragments into independent fiefdoms under the rule of rival warlords. Paradise lost.

Three important conclusions flow from this analysis. The first is that you can't indulge in a major programme of redistribution and welfare before you have experienced a period of high economic growth. That is why democratic welfare should come towards the end of the "High Road" trajectory. You have to earn the money before you spend it. The second implication is that trade unions should be as interested in a positive outcome as business, because there is no authoritarian regime anywhere in the world that tolerates trade unions. If the country slides into a "failure of growth" scenario, Cosatu will suffer along with everybody else. Indeed, the history of the twentieth century has shown the dangers for everyone of a nation entering a period of general wretchedness. Both Mussolini and Hitler were elected by the unemployed to improve their lot.

The third point is that we have been very lucky to have Nelson Mandela as our president, because he has legendary status and has acted as the glue to hold the country together. But as a legend, he is irreplaceable. So the glue has to change. "The High Road" assumes that when Nelson Mandela goes, the glue that holds the country together is economic success. In all other "winning nations" in the world, people are not overly worried about who the leader is, as they are too busy creating wealth for themselves and their families. In our case, success will also blur the old lines of colour, ethnicity and language, since individuals will see themselves as part of the winning rainbow team.

·

When Mandela Goes

Let's hope Lester's pessimistic scenario doesn't materialise. But the buck stops with each and every one of us to create a better scenario.

26.10.1997 Wham! What happens after Mandela? That is the subject of a thoughtful book by Lester Venter entitled *When Mandela Goes*.

The scenario he sketches is that Mbeki succeeds Mandela as leader and wins the 1999 election. However, the economy flounders afterwards and a Cosatu/SACP alliance splits from the ANC to form Anlap – the African National Labour Party. With increasing unrest among the masses caused by a perceived lack of delivery on the part of the ANC, Anlap is elected as the new government in 2004 on the basis that it – unlike the ANC – will lead us to the promised land.

Is this scenario credible? It all depends on how the economy actually performs. Because of the economic state we're in, apparently there has already been a marked increase in floating voters whose allegiance is up for grabs. History certainly demonstrates that anything can happen in a country where the national misery index soars on account of a malfunctioning economy. Thus, the Venter scenario has precedents. Indeed, he also quotes an important conclusion of the Nedcor scenario exercise in his favour: no country has ever made a successful transition to an open democratic society without an appropriate level of economic growth to accompany it. Political and economic liberty go hand in hand.

While Venter is careful not to suggest that our preciously won democracy is going to be extinguished, he is venturing that the country will lurch to the left for a while after 2004. So the obvious question is: what level of annual growth in the South African economy is necessary to pre-empt the Venter scenario and keep the ANC in power? Current economic models imply that growth of 3 to 4 per cent per annum is not good enough – unemployment will still increase. The growth rate has to rise to something in the range of 6 to 8 per cent per annum for a better life for all to begin to be a reality in the squatter camps and townships where the ANC's main support base exists.

Well, I can hear readers say, that goes to show that Venter's analysis is spot on since we only came close to a growth rate of that magnitude in the fifties and sixties when inflation was 2½ per cent and the gold mines were getting into full swing. I'm inclined not to be so negative. For a start, our economy hit 6 per cent per annum economic growth in the bad old days when the handbrake of apartheid was fully on and the vast majority were being actively excluded from any form of wealth creation. Imagine if the whole process is reversed and we actively include the masses in the process of wealth creation. Imagine if the ANC make it their top priority to create a favourable environment in which a new entrepreneurial class flourishes in the townships.

Before you dismiss these "wild imaginings" just remember that the world economy is in a long boom to the year 2020, fuelled by the latest advances in information technology and genetic engineering. In other words, we have a following overseas wind. Remember too that the African renaissance in Uganda, Tanzania, Zambia and Malawi is all about reducing the role of the state and letting the private sector get on with it. The "winds of change" are blowing on our continent too. And remember how cynical many were ten years ago about a negotiated political settlement. The unthinkable sometimes happens. Twice in our lifetime isn't out of sight!

Now have I got you in a different frame of mind? Maybe, then, there'll be no rude awakening for the ANC. But what Venter confirms is that it's better for the ANC to aim high and miss the target than aim low and hit it.

Christopher Columbus
Oh for passionate leaders to steer us in a new direction!

11.10.1998 In an article last year, I mentioned the top ten most admired companies in America as compiled by *Fortune* magazine. This year's list contains six of last year's names: Microsoft, Coca-Cola, Intel, Berkshire Hathaway, Johnson & Johnson and Merck. The four newcomers are General Electric – straight in at no. 1 – with Hewlett Packard, Southwest Airlines and Disney listed elsewhere.

If you'd invested $1 000 into each of these companies' stock on 31 December 1987 – and reinvested the dividends you'd received – you'd have been sitting on $146 419 at the end of 1997. That's a compound annual return of 31 per cent compared to the average for the market as a whole of just under 18 per cent. Pretty mind-blowing stuff!

Whilst citing a variety of factors for the success of these companies, *Fortune* this year singles out one as crucial – leadership. Warren Buffett, himself the leader of Berkshire Hathaway, believes that people vote for the artist, not the painting. But what are the common characteristics of the CEOs of the top ten? Certainly not their personalities or their management styles. All ten are their own men.

Professor John Kotter of the Harvard Business School has done a fascinating analysis and offers three uniform features of top leaders, while *Fortune* adds two of its own. Kotter's first finding is that leaders help a group establish some sensible direction. Buffett says: "Vision is too fancy, but they (the CEOs) have a dream and the dream isn't fleshed out, which is why they are never satisfied."

The second constant of great leaders, according to Kotter, is getting the relevant partners aligned with, buying into and believing in the direction they set. This is not so much to do with specific results but the broader idea of what the company should be and why. They're tireless at putting this idea across, whether it's in informal conversations in the corridors, in formal presentations at conferences or in the annual report of the company. They focus on nothing else.

Kotter's third asset of a leader is quintessentially American: the ability to create conditions that energise and inspire people to get off their backsides and do it. Need one say more? The fourth attribute as supplied by *Fortune* is a knack for allocating capital. This is half discipline and half art. In the opinion of one expert, Alfred Rappaport, leaders "have an economic model that makes sense, that they understand, which they use as a navigational tool. They don't have a whole bunch of measures."

Last but not least, *Fortune* states that "great business leaders ought to reveal all the traits of a great lover – passion, commitment, ferocity. Nothing less will do." Buffett supports this: "I could play golf like Tiger Woods but if Berkshire were not doing well, I'd not be happy."

Looking over these five characteristics, I'm struck by the similarity between great leaders and a great explorer like Christopher Columbus. He had a broad sense of where he wanted to go even though his knowledge of the globe was rudimentary and he ended up somewhere else. He aligned all his sponsors to put up sufficient funds to set out on the voyage. He certainly got his crew to do it. He juggled what money he had to buy the provisions to get him there. And he had a burning passion to explore. The net result: he discovered America!

Carpe Diem

All of us need to seize the day like Peter Gush did during his life.

31.5.1998 The book opens. On a crisp Highveld morning exactly two weeks ago, people arrive at St Saviour's Church at Randjesfontein for the christening of Kira Susan Baptiste. As the Presbyterian minister splashes water on her face, I think of all the scenarios that may unfold for that little person.

Will she grow up to be a teacher like her mother, a computer whizz like her father, or a cup-winning basketball player like both of them? Perhaps her mixture of genes will produce an entirely different individual who, to the surprise of her parents, becomes an ardent feminist, a famed writer or a beautiful actress. Who knows, as the minister gazes into those liquid little eyes and blesses her? The mystery lies ahead.

The book closes and, between its covers, the multiple pathways of the future turn into the single track of the past. Two days later, in a marquee at the Johannesburg Country Club, I along with many other people mourn the death of Edwin Peter Gush. EPG was a brilliant colleague of mine in Anglo. He obtained a mining degree at Wits, worked underground, gained a Rhodes scholarship to Oxford, managed a blue in both rowing and rugby, and ascended up the Anglo hierarchy like a rocket to be on the Executive Committee by his mid-thirties. With an immense appetite for work, he left big footprints in business wherever he went.

Yet, listening to the moving tributes from his children, I realised what a fine family man he must have been as well. My favourite memory of Peter was surfing some huge waves with him at Plettenberg Bay. In the fading afternoon sunlight, he admonished me roundly for using a board. He regarded it as a soft option, but there was no way that I was going to ride those waves unassisted!

My mother recently moved into a smaller abode and was getting rid of the bulk of her possessions. I managed to save all the old photographs she'd accumulated over the years from both her and my father's side of the family. I keep them in a trunk at home and occasionally sift through them.

There's a picture of my three uncles all in their top hats and tails as contemporary schoolboys at Eton College. There's my mother in the ball gown she wore for her coming-out party. There's my father spruced up in his army uniform as he leads my mother out of the church on their wedding day during the Second World War. There's me in my swimsuit reconnoitring a narrow gangplank as part of a preparatory school obstacle race. Snapshots certainly compress life into a brief series of hellos and goodbyes. But that's the way it is.

As I write this article, I hear the Reverend Granville Morgan's sonorous Welsh voice when he opens the memorial service for Peter: "The nature of God is a circle of which the centre is everywhere and the circumference is nowhere." Life has boundless opportunities. *Carpe diem.* Seize the day, for tomorrow we're gone.

Small is Beautiful

It is essential for us to develop a whole new approach to small business. I believe that the franchise system can play a major role in this area; for the franchisor brings to the relationship not only an established brand name, but also a proven modus operandi, management control systems, back-up support and buying power. Moreover, the franchisee receives comprehensive and ongoing multidisciplinary training to enable him or her to manage a sustainable business. The chances of failure are therefore substantially reduced.

8.4.1998 If the proposed job summit is to be a success, it must start from one inescapable premise. Neither the public service in South Africa nor the top 100 companies will be major job creators over the next ten years. One could argue that in both sectors there may actually be net job destruction. On the one hand the civil service is targeted to slim down from 1,5 million to around 1,2 million employees; and, on the other hand globalisation and new technologies will mean big business inevitably producing more products and services with fewer people. In the latter area, though, you could argue that major new projects by local and foreign investors will add to the workforce. However, one is usually talking of several thousand people per project, which is a drop in the ocean compared to the six or seven million new jobs required. Ah, you may say, but there is a multiplier effect. Fine, that will help the medium-sized business, small business and informal sectors where I contend the primary focus of the summit should be.

Nor is South Africa out of step with international trends. Some 95 per cent of the new jobs generated in economies around the world are in companies of less than 200 people; and the *Fortune 500* companies in America have been net job destroyers over the last ten years. Indeed, they've shed millions of jobs. As Judie Lannon, adviser to our London scenario team maintains, we are moving into a fragmented, postmodernist society where the nature of work and employment is changing. The average size of the workforce in the public and private sectors alike is declining everywhere. Humpty Dumpty will never be put back together again. The summit must accept this.

Given the above analysis, I am fairly dubious about any public works programme devised by the government to mop up un-employment. All it will do is put pressure on the government to meet the budget deficit targets set out in GEAR, drive up interest rates and slow down economic growth. A counter-argument may be put forward that the programme will be funded by savings made elsewhere in the budget. But that will inevitably mean laying off even more civil servants. So you give with the one hand and take with the other. The net effect is zero. I'm sorry – Keynes has had his day. We have to move on.

I believe that we have to destroy the myth that if big govern-ment, big business and big labour get together they can some-how pull a rabbit out of the hat and create millions of new jobs. It just isn't going to happen that way. Rather, it will be because we create a climate conducive for existing entrepreneurs to grow their businesses and for new entrepreneurs to open up addi-tional enterprises. Hence, I have been advocating for some time that the focus of the RDP should be changed from home owner-ship to the creation of a new entrepreneurial class in South Africa. The reason for promoting this is that joblessness is more fundamental than homelessness. If a person has a job, he can buy a house; but if he doesn't have a job, even if you give him a house he can't maintain it. To me, it would be a marvellous way of revitalising the RDP and allowing the private sector, in part-nership with the government, to construct realistic action pro-grammes to achieve the new goal. To this end, the forthcoming summit should be called an enterprise summit, rather than a job summit. It is only through the creation of millions of enterprises that we will create millions of jobs.

Over the dinner table the other night, a young black business-man put the challenge superbly. He said we had to turn nineteenth-century capitalism into 21st-century capitalism. He affirmed that most blacks thought of capitalism as the nineteenth-century variety where you had a few bosses and millions of slaves – in other words, a system of oppression. What we have to do is jump 100 years to 21st century-capitalism which consists of a network of small business entrepreneurs all doing their own thing, getting a lot of fun and amusement out of it and, at the same time, obtaining self-esteem and dignity. This type of capitalism would be seen as a liberating experience. I think there is a lot in what he says. Incidentally, therefore, the idea of public works programmes would only re-enforce the paradigm of nineteenth-century capitalism as it will do nothing to raise the self-esteem of the youth involved. It would merely be a way of giving them some form of employment for money – and not much money at that.

In the light of these arguments, I have for some months been proposing certain actions to help to create an entrepreneurial society. One of the principal bottlenecks that I have identified is lack of access to equity capital for small business people (particularly in the townships). The JSE is prohibitively expensive though they're looking to change into something more relevant for the emerging business sector. Nevertheless, I would like to see a network of regional stock exchanges, which specialise in over-the-counter stocks and flotation of small businesses. One can use the latest system of computerised, screen-based trading with no scrip in order to minimise transaction costs. Nasdaq, in the US, is a superb example, and has the highest level of initial public offerings in the world. At the time that it was established, many Americans felt that there was no place for a second stock exchange as well as the New York Stock Exchange. But they have been proved completely wrong as volumes on Nasdaq are similar to those on the NYSE. So why not sprinkle some Sasdaqs around South Africa?

It is such a shame that we are obsessed with the granting of casino licences when we should be channelling the national gambling instinct into stock exchanges of this kind. Casinos are programmed for people to lose. All that is going to happen is that the savings of the masses are going to end up in the hands of a few casino owners (especially seeing that 70-80 per cent of a casino's takings come from slot machines). At least regional stock exchanges would be neutral, although one has to accept that simplification of the rules could lead to a greater possibility of scams.

However, a critical point is that equity capital should be the fundamental source of capital for small businesses, not loan capital. We all know that gearing risky projects 100 per cent is a dumb idea in big business, so that conclusion has equal validity for small business. Yet there seems to be an attitude around in this country that the only source of capital for small business should be loan finance from the SBDC, the NGOs who run start-up funds or the banks. But remember that the main reason for the collapse of the Asian markets was business expansion based on credit. When growth slowed, the flaws in this approach immediately became apparent. The other side of the coin is that banks here are constantly criticised for not doing more for small business. But they simply don't possess the risk profile to lend large sums of money to small business. They're lending depositors' money – not their own – and the latter would be extremely upset if they suffered losses as a result of bad debts to the bank. At best, they can provide wholesale finance to microlending agencies, which specialise in this field, and thereby reduce their risk.

From the point of view of the person wanting the money and the person wanting to invest, therefore, venture capital makes more sense than loan capital. Indeed, realistically, it would be venture capital companies with a portfolio of township businesses that would be quoted on the stock exchanges rather than individual township stocks. Old Mutual isn't going to invest in a single spaza shop. An alternative is to modify the existing stokvel system so that members' subscriptions are invested in a range of businesses owned by the members. Stokvels could even be turned into closed stock exchanges if members started trading in each other's shares.

In promoting the idea of regional stock exchanges in places like Durban and Cape Town, I make the point that the Johannesburg Stock Exchange in the 1880s wasn't that well regulated and firms of accountants were not auditing the financial statements of those early companies. Equally, when a prospector went into a bar waving a claim in front of the guys drinking there, he would say: "If you each put £10 into my prospect and we hit gold you will make a fortune; if we don't hit gold you lose your £10." That was the prospectus – end of story!

Yet another reason for the stock exchange proposal is that the media would suddenly start talking about township businesses and entrepreneurs instead of ignoring them completely as they do at the moment. Right now the masses have the impression that the content of the media is written by the elite for the elite about the elite. Trading of stocks and shares on a much wider basis would act as a catalyst to overcome this problem.

Should you still not be convinced that this idea will run, there is a halfway house. It's something the Australian Stock Exchange is doing. Why not set up a market site on the Internet which can act as a matchmaker between venture capitalists wanting to invest on the one hand and small businesses needing the capital on the other? The deals can be consummated off screen in private. Internet cafes are already popping up in the townships.

The second recommendation I have for an entrepreneurial society is entrepreneurial education in schools. This isn't talk-and-chalk stuff, but a programme for kids to open up real businesses on school premises and also in the adjoining towns. The Wykeham Collegiate School for Girls in Pietermaritzburg is an illustration of what can be done. They start training the girls at the age of nine, so that by the time they are eighteen they are seasoned entrepreneurs. Obviously, there should also be adult entrepreneurial training centres in the townships and elsewhere. A wonderful example, although it is about to be closed down for lack of funds, has been a business advisory centre operated by the University of Potchefstroom in Tembisa.

The third proposal I have is the establishment of chairs of entrepreneurship at major universities and technikons. I am glad to say that Rhodes University and Port Elizabeth Technikon have decided to set up such a chair jointly. The University of Pretoria already has one. But I also know that there are many others who would do so if they had the money. Such chairs should be used not only to provide courses on entrepreneurship at tertiary institutions for students, but also to act as centres of research into the small business and informal sectors. We are woefully ignorant of what goes on in the township economies at the moment.

For example, I went into a shack the other day where the shack owner was hiring out to the local community five cellulars chained to a concrete block. His monthly takings are between R10 000 and R20 000 on a capital employed of around R1 000. So the returns are much higher than in big business. On another occasion I had lunch with a Soweto loan shark who responded as follows when I mentioned that 20 per cent per annum was a high interest rate: "Get wise, Clem, I charge 50 per cent a month and when times are tight, 100 per cent a weekend. I will give you R100 on Friday, but you pay me back R200 on Monday or else a special system of peer pressure comes into play!"

Have you ever seen an article in any newspaper or journal or academic treatise detailing the world of shack businesses and loan sharking? The answer is no. But how can you have sound policy recommendations without sound comment and research?

The fourth proposal is that government needs to look at its own role in creating a conducive climate for entrepreneurs. Steps needing consideration include money in the RDP fund being set aside for investment in emerging business or to guarantee investments by private financial institutions in that sector; a corporation tax holiday for businesses up to a certain size (or even graduated corporation tax like graduated income tax); minimising regulations to start up and run a small business; a one-stop licence issuing shop; specific law and order measures to protect small businesses which are all cash-based; roads for rural businesses to get their product to market; and outsourcing as many current activities done by the state at national, provincial and local level to small business as possible. This is precisely what President Museveni of Uganda is doing. He has gone to the people and asked them what they need to assist them in running their businesses and has prioritised government expenditure accordingly. He comes from the new generation of leaders who have shrugged off the past and are focused on the future. He is the African renaissance.

The last idea I have is that we should have a medal awarded by the State President each month to an outstanding entrepreneur. We need some form of hype from the government in order to elevate the status of entrepreneurs in the minds of the public. Unfortunately, South Africa has inherited the European attitude to entrepreneurs as opposed to the American attitude. The European attitude is epitomised by the large country mansions in England where you have a front entrance and a tradesmen's entrance. Trade, or the entrepreneur, is considered so inferior that he is not allowed to knock on the front door. This attitude permeates our society where entrepreneurs are well behind politicians, lawyers, academics and others in the public's mind. In fact, they are perceived almost akin to criminals. By contrast, in America – in places like California – they are given the same kind of hero worship as major sports stars. A guy beavering away in his garage in Silicon Valley making a new chip which will knock Andy Grove, head of Intel, off his perch, is regarded in the same light as Michael Jordan, the ace basketball player. New money is just as good as old money, while in Europe new money is dismissed as nouveau riche.

I hope you, the reader, have captured the spirit in which I am putting forward these fairly revolutionary ideas. Somehow, we should use the job (or may I say enterprise) summit to turn the paradigm about small business upside down, as it will be the crucible for job creation in the foreseeable future. I am not for one moment saying that the top 100 companies in South Africa are not also going to play a vital role in economic growth, but they simply aren't going to create the jobs.

VSMEs
We need to bring down the price of money.

30.8.1998 Suppose you're in a café, you take a two-litre container of Coca-Cola out of the fridge and you ask the proprietor at the counter how much it is. In response, he asks, "How much are you worth?" Slightly surprised by this rather impertinent question, you reply, "Well, actually, I'm a company director so I'm pretty well off." He says, "That's fine, I'll give you a 10 per cent discount on the official price of R8,00 so you can have it for R7,20." Even more surprised, you hand over the money.

As you do so, out of the corner of your eye you see another

guy heading from the fridge to the counter with a similar quantity of Coke. His down-at-heel appearance and five-day stubble suggest that he's not in the same wealth league as you are. The proprietor asks him the identical question about worth. His response is different to yours: "Man, I'm strung out. I've spent the last few months trying to start my own business. I don't want charity but it would be nice to have a break. But I guess you'd say I'm poor at the moment." "In that case," says the proprietor, "I'm going to have to charge you double the normal price, so that will be R16,00 please." As the relatively richer of the two, you are nonplussed. How can he be charged more when he has the greater need? You shake your head as you go out.

Now switch to a bank and change the product in demand from Coke to money. The scene you witnessed in the café is taking place every day in the bank. In fact, if you're a customer below a certain threshold of poverty, you won't be able to obtain the product from the bank at any price, i.e. any rate of interest. You'll have to go to a "shylock" – township slang for a loan shark – who'll charge you fifty times the normal price of money (equivalent to R400 for the Coke).

Of course, there's a perfectly good reason for a bank to behave differently to a café. They're taking a risk in selling you the money because after a certain period of time they want it back. And the poorer you are, the less likely you are to pay it back. Hence, on the logically unimpeachable principle that reward should rise commensurately with risk, the price of money is higher for the poor than the rich. The banks will argue that they have to be risk averse since most of the money they're lending isn't their money; it belongs to the public. The poor will respond that banks only lend money to people who don't need it anyway.

So it all depends on your frame of reference, as modern physicists would say. When they do an experiment to prove that light is a wave, it behaves like a wave. When they do an experiment to prove that it is a particle, it behaves like a particle. What you see is what you get. Likewise, bankers are being perfectly consistent within their frame of reference while poor people feel wronged in theirs.

But an imaginative solution has to be found to this capital log jam. It became clear at a recent conference on alternative means of finance that VSMEs (very small and micro-enterprises seeking loans of anything up to R100 000) should be distinguished from SMEs (small and medium-sized enterprises seeking loans in excess of R100 000). While the latter have relatively easy access to capital from banks, NGOs and venture capital funds, the former have fewer ports of call. Moreover, these are considerably more expensive not only because of the risk but also because of the sheer cost of administering a microcredit portfolio. As someone at the conference remarked, it's easier as a micro guy in South Africa to get a loan for consumption than production.

I have been proposing for some time that a portion of RDP money should be set aside as a guarantee fund. This would serve to underpin loans from the private sector to VSMEs. As such, with much less risk involved for the bank, interest rates to VSMEs could be much lower. In fact, armed with a government guarantee, VSMEs become triple-A borrowers entitled to the best price for money the market can offer. Since VSMEs are probably the most powerful vehicle for job creation around, their multiplication and growth are the best means for government to achieve the GEAR employment targets. It should make them think, shouldn't it?

Khula

So, how do we facilitate greater access to credit and equity capital for VSMEs? Enter Khula.

6.9.1998 As Minister of Trade and Industry, Alec Erwin has three aces in his hand which he can put on the table any time. They are Sizwe Tati, Estelle Duvenage and Anne Hilton. Sizwe is MD of Khula Enterprise Finance Ltd and Estelle and Anne are senior employees in Khula Credit Guarantee Ltd, a wholly owned subsidiary of Khula Enterprise Finance.

Because of my interest in access to finance for the small business sector, I have met all three and have been most impressed.

Khula means "grow" in Xhosa and the companies bearing the name are anything but plodding state organisations.

Khula was established in 1996 as a result of the President's Conference on Small Business. Its mission is to provide capital and expertise to this sector. It generally does not invest directly in the small business applicant, but aids the growing network of outlets which are categorised as Retail Financial Intermediaries (RFIs) that deal with the public. These include banks, NGOs and provincial development corporations. Khula's financing activities are divided into the following: loans of between R1 million and R100 million to existing RFIs with the express provision that the money is on-lent to small business; seed loans for new RFIs targeting this market; capacity building of RFIs, including the design of debtor systems and training of loan officers; joint equity funding with RFIs of small businesses with a net asset value in excess of R500 000; and credit guarantees to the RFIs in respect of individual loans to small businesses or for an RFI's entire portfolio of loans to this sector (Khula will also provide guarantees to banks who lend to NGOs who in turn lend to micro-entrepreneurs). These guarantees are for up to 80 per cent of the money lent.

Since lack of expertise and experience are two major constraints on small business obtaining capital, Khula is also setting up a mentorship programme to run in tandem with its financing activities. The mentor will assist not only in formulating the business plan, but also in the loan application and the subsequent running of the enterprise. Khula is in the process of accrediting mentors for this scheme. The kind of people they are looking for are active, retired or semiretired people from a variety of backgrounds – entrepreneurial, management, import/export, legal/financial/procurements, business start-ups, manufacturing and service sectors such as textiles, catering and construction and professions like engineering and quantity surveying.

To streamline loan applications to RFIs, Khula is setting up a new initiative to pre-evaluate applications and issue up to 80 per cent guarantees. The entrepreneur can then submit the application to the bank with a guarantee in place upfront. This process is to be implemented in six centres around the country in the next few months. Nine banks are already participating in the credit guarantee scheme and Khula hopes to get more involved.

At the moment Khula is capitalised at R308 million and has approved 2 560 guarantees totalling R126 million. The bad debt claims against the guarantees are below 5 per cent, indicating that most small businesses are not as high a risk as is generally perceived. Personally, I believe that Khula should receive the same priority as law and order in Cabinet circles. It represents the long-term arm of the government for stabilising society. Ultimately, Khula should be capitalised at billions of rand when it is fully resourced to handle that kind of money.

The Other Comrades Marathon

Beating poverty is not for sissies who give up easily. One of the people who attended the poverty summit, Margaret Legum, subsequently reminded me of the important role "social entrepreneurs" can play in communities. They have the same sort of skills as economic entrepreneurs – bringing together people with resources and solutions with needs, matching skills to roles, and above all providing intelligent energy. The difference between the two breeds is that the social version is not interested in profit. They ask to be paid with a modest but reasonable salary; but their chief driving force is to make a difference in a community. They want to be remembered, and they want to see many people much better off for their work.

It is only in the last few years that they have been recognised as a valuable human resource. Some research in the UK suggests that, per unit of capital invested in them, they create ten times the number of income-bearing jobs that economic entrepreneurs do. The possible reason for this success in terms of creating local economies is that social entrepreneurs are not making fine calculations about profits and rates of return to shareholders; they are interested only in getting something done that will last.

19.7.1998 "Comrades, or may I say, fellow long-distance runners in the race against poverty." It was a nice touch from Professor Francis Wilson of the University of Cape Town to remind us that there are no short cuts to uprooting poverty. Anybody who joins up does so for the long haul.

We were all gathered together at Escom's Midrand Training Centre for the recent poverty summit organised by the churches. Wilson's speech contained two other telling pieces of advice. Firstly, we're past playing the blame game and piling up a whole list of "oughts" for other people to do. It's now a case of what we personally can do to help. Secondly, research into poverty should lead directly to action rather than displace it. Bluntly, I took this to mean that academics should stop being academic, roll up their sleeves and be relevant to the objects of their research.

The Anglican Archbishop of Cape Town, the Most Reverend Njongonkulu Ndungane, echoed this statement in his opening address: "Words, words and more words – they don't feed the poor. We need to move from words to action. We now require an active partnership between government, the labour movement and the private sector, as well as religious and NGO sectors, and other organs of civil society, to work hand in hand to ensure that we put in place *attainable, sustainable and measurable* strategies to eradicate poverty." The italics are mine because these three adjectives succinctly sum up the way we should approach anti-poverty programmes.

A similarly impassioned but realistic plea was made by Rams Ramashia, President of the South African NGO Coalition (Sangoco). "The opportunity is not yet lost but time is ticking away. The time will come when no eloquent political rhetoric will quench the anger of the poor. However, their expectations are actually so modest that we should be ashamed that they are not met. People are not expecting highly paid jobs, company cars, flushing toilets, tarred roads and street lights. What they are expecting is the opportunity to send their children to school, to have containers filled with water so they don't have to walk miles every day and to have land to work on." In short, the poverty hearings conducted around the country revealed that the poor don't want everything now. On the contrary, they want to know that the country is setting off down a path where one by one their problems are going to be addressed. Long-term sustainability should not be sacrificed for short-term expediency.

Dr Pundy Pillay from the Deputy President's Office pointed out that antipoverty strategies in developing countries had two predominant objectives: a growth-oriented economic policy to increase employment and the provision of basic social services as a safety net. In order to identify the proper targets in the latter regard, it was necessary to measure the extent and intensity of poverty. Often the poorest of the poor were neglected because programmes were too universal, i.e. they offered assistance to many people who didn't really need it. He stressed that the Malaysian experience showed it takes time to conquer the problem. He also indicated that government should no longer be considered a major source of job creation. Thus, welfare initiatives would have to be structured in such a way that they were not hand-outs to passive recipients but a source of empowerment which led people to take charge of their own lives.

What I really liked about these opening addresses was the philosophical foundation they laid for the rest of the conference (and for the forthcoming job summit as well). Basically, don't look for quick fixes because even the poor don't expect them; don't waste time any more with rhetoric but concentrate only on ideas that can easily lead to action; and help people to help themselves.

Next week, I'll talk about some of the practical proposals that emerged from the summit.

Sunday Sermons
We should call on the churches to help.

26.7.1998 At the recent poverty summit, I acted as facilitator for a fascinating breakaway group made up of powerful individuals from diverse backgrounds. Nevertheless, they had one thing in common – a desire for the summit not to be just another summit but one that had the potential for practical follow-through. Ideas came thick and fast – from the left, right and centre – so I had no trouble reporting back to the plenary session at the end.

The first suggestion made in our breakaway session was that in terms of service delivery to the poor, each role player's responsibility should be clarified. Specifically, three questions should be asked: to whom is the service provided, how should it be provided and who should do it? Responsibilities should subsequently be allocated to the various agencies according to their energy and competence.

The second thought was that dialogue between service providers and clients (the poor) should be improved, because both the public and private sectors are guilty of pursuing their own agendas and often doing things that the poor see no sense in. The poor should therefore be active participants in poverty reduction programmes. Moreover, young people who are existing champions of projects to alleviate poverty in rural communities should be identified and trained as development officers at urban tertiary institutions and then be posted back. Generally, it was essential to discover the energy already present in the community and enhance it.

Related to the second point, all the programmes within the social security ambit should be scrutinised to see what impact they have on the family, and whether they add to or subtract from the initiative and self-sufficiency of the community. The indicators of success to judge the merit of such programmes ought to be output- and not input-oriented. The kind of questions to raise include: are the programmes demand driven, will the results be sustainable in the long run and are they relevant to the special needs of the poorest communities who live well off the main road?

Then we dealt specifically with the contribution which should be sought from all religious denominations in the country. Given the widespread ignorance amongst the poor about programmes that have been set up to assist them, it was felt that the church in each community should act as an information centre in this regard. The church has a network second to none and every Sunday is a golden opportunity to brief parishioners on initiatives to combat poverty. The church can also act as an effective two-way communication link – on the one hand for national agencies to get their message down to grassroots and, on the other, for grassroots organisations to be heard at the top. The church has the added advantage of having no political affiliations that might distort the message. In addition, church land and property should be put to optimal use in servicing the needs of the poor.

Our group believed strongly that the churches as well as other faith communities need to rekindle a sense of morality in our society. They should proclaim a new moral vision, which will help to stamp out crime and corruption and revive civic responsibility. Moreover, church schools are probably the most effectively run institutions (as in America) for talented but poverty-stricken kids to rise above the grind. So the government here should be going out of its way to support these schools instead of cutting their subsidies.

On a lighter note, one of the better comments to come out of the final plenary session of the summit was the following: "The church is there not only to comfort the afflicted but also to afflict the comfortable." It lends new meaning to the phrase "no peace for the wicked".

Poverty FM

Poverty has to be attacked from all sides. I'll add one suggestion to kick off the programme. What about every single business in this country adopting one entrepreneur?

2.8.1998 I mentioned some ideas last week that came out of our breakaway group at the poverty summit. Here are some more.

Tendering procedures should be simplified so that both the government and private sector can award more contracts to microbusinesses; the poor and unemployed should have direct representation on the National Development Agency to make it more sensitive to their needs; they should attend Nedlac meetings when their affairs are being discussed and be a principal player at the forthcoming job summit; traditional structures in rural areas should be targeted to improve their attitude to gender equality and to overcome the difficulty of land ownership for women; intracommunity networks which encourage the purchase and sale of local produce through a system of debits and credits should be established (examples of local energy transfer systems already operate in Australia); each community should have a forum designed to reduce overlap between churches, NGOs and government bodies in their fight against poverty; student exchange programmes with overseas NGOs involved in poverty alleviation should be expanded and best practice internationally in the upliftment of poor people should be explored.

On the media front, books should be published with stories of local and overseas poverty beaters; more programmes should be aired on radio/TV on ways out of poverty (what about a Poverty radio station?); a rural version of Soul City should be screened; an Internet site for people to exchange ideas on escaping poverty might be feasible if computer companies could wire up the whole of South Africa; more publicity should be given to the prevention of HIV and AIDS which affect the poor the most; and above all the press generally should launch a "can-do" campaign featuring challenges rather than problems and giving two principal messages – we can move beyond poverty (it is not an endless swamp) and what can I do about it?

The business sector should provide mentors to assist the poor in developing a spirit of self-sufficiency (especially making it part of the management education programme for talented young people earmarked for the top and calling on the services of "grey power" – pensioners who have years of experience); they should fund NGOs who are adopting best practice in each niche of poverty reduction (which means some form of performance measurement); they should, wherever possible, establish franchise operations because these have the best chance of becoming sustainable businesses in the long run; they should help in the crucial function of marketing, as this is always a weak area for poor communities; and they should be asked to declare the percentage of their profits allocated to social responsibility programmes (giving rise to garlands or brickbats).

The group also agreed on the necessity to provide adult literacy/ numeracy programmes to the poor through distance education (radiating from a central studio to a network of satellite classrooms and allowing for interaction between teacher and pupil); business advisory centres in each community offering advice on a wide range of occupational options and on where to get capital; and perhaps a one-year national service for young people to combat poverty.

Looking back, we brainstormed lots of ideas in our little group. Now comes the hard part of turning as many of them as possible into action, as poverty will only be beaten by attacking it simultaneously on every front.

The Boot

Here are eight steps to give poverty the boot. This was my contribution to the poverty summit.

27.6.1998 The eight steps for communities to escape poverty are:

* *Focus.* Focus is the only way to turn great ideas into action. The Americans have the slogan, "Ready, fire, aim". Ours is "Ready, aim, have another conference, aim, have another workshop, aim . . ." We never pull the trigger and fire.

* *Differentiation.* We must differentiate ourselves in some way, either by producing an original product or by offering a special service, or by powerful branding. There is a need to develop coherent African brands that set our products apart from those of America, Europe and the East. If we think of rural development, we must ask what each community is able to produce which is different and which can take advantage of African branding.

* *Benchmarking.* We need to benchmark ourselves against best practice in the rest of the world, particularly when we examine ways of steering capital to very small and micro-enterprises. Experience has shown that financial support is available in South Africa for small to medium-sized enter-

prises (those with capital of R100 000 and more), but not for very small enterprises. The Grameen Bank in Bangladesh is a good example of an institution that we can copy to fill this gap. We must have the self-confidence to feel that we can perform to the best standards in the world.

* *A perpetual spirit of innovation.* Innovation is not the preserve of the top echelon in organisations. A positive environment must be created in which everyone has the confidence to come forward with new ideas. We are a rule-bound society – ordinary people are fearful of promoting their own ideas. People must stop fearing that they will be made to look stupid in front of their peers.

* *Flexibility.* Communities must be flexible in the face of changes in the market. Moreover, markets change suddenly, not slowly, and communities should be in a position to adapt to what the market requires, and have a sensitive "radar system" to work this out.

* *Ability to attract, develop and retain talented young people.* The provision of education of a high standard is the key to fulfilling this objective. If communities want to keep their talented young people, then they are going to have to provide the climate in which those young people will stay and use their creative spirit to build local economies around their villages.

* *Social and environmental responsibility.* Consumers now look behind the products that they are buying to see whether they are comfortable with the ethics of the producer. Communities will have to demonstrate their commitment to high norms of social, environmental and civic responsibility if they are to be successful in the marketplace.

* *Leadership.* Communities need champions who believe passionately in the future of their communities and inspire others around them to make things happen.

33

Homeless Talk
We need to teach the homeless to help themselves.

15.2.1998 At the bottom left-hand side of the front page appear the words: "Please buy from badged, bibbed and sober sellers only." The subtitle of the paper is "Helping the homeless help themselves". The title is *Homeless Talk*.

I buy a copy every month though I confess I don't check the breath of the seller as I hand over the money. It was at first a guilt-buy. But, after reading a few issues, I am genuinely taken by the articles, letters and poems crammed into its sixteen pages. It officially costs R2 of which R1,20 goes to the seller and 80c to the paper. In practice, people pay whatever they have in their pocket and I've heard that one person on principle forks out R100. The experienced sellers position themselves at choice spots like the traffic lights at Hyde Park and Sandton City. There are some 500 distributors on the street. The earnings of the really successful ones exceed R300 per month and four actually notch up R2 000.

The sellers, writers and administrative staff of the paper are mainly drawn from the ranks of the homeless (of which 15 000 live in the Johannesburg CBD). In particular, the writers portray life on the wrong side of the tracks with a vividness you won't find anywhere else in the South African media. Interestingly, more than two-thirds of the readers of *Homeless Talk* come from the top two national income groups. It goes to show that the elite really do hanker after knowing more about the problems facing their less fortunate brethren. Moreover, they prefer to support people who are helping themselves than the bearers of cardboard messages just begging for assistance.

All personnel are trained at the Bree Street offices of the paper. Courses include accounting, marketing, writing and photographic skills. A substantial portion of the costs is met by sponsorship and donations. Glenn Grant, the paper's co-ordinator, is mainly responsible for the rise in its circulation to the current level of 30 000 a month. He proudly says there are no returns from the print run. The sellers ensure that every paper gets sold.

His background is varied. It includes schooling at Jeppe Boys High, motorcycle racing, launching radio stations in Vienna and the US and the publication of a golfing journal. His stated intention is to turn the paper into a national fortnightly issue with regional content tailored to each major city.

Recently, I've been advocating that the RDP should be given a different focus. Instead of providing direct grants to homeless people to help them get homes, the focus should be on the creation of a new entrepreneurial class who create jobs for themselves and thereby earn enough so that they can afford homes. The result will be a lot more self-sustaining and bring much greater satisfaction to the individuals concerned.

Listen to Betty Tshabalala whose article was contained in a recent edition of the paper. "Since I started selling *Homeless Talk* my life is different in terms of finance. I currently manage to maintain myself with everything. I pay my rent which is R200 a month. I buy groceries of more than R150 a month. Before I sold *Homeless Talk*, my life was a misery. I was eating at the help-centres and churches. I was staying in a women's shelter at 80 Albert Street. I am 42 but now I feel strong like a young woman."

If the RDP were redirected towards helping all the folk like Betty to fulfil their innate potential, South Africa would be a better place. We must recognise that joblessness is more fundamental than homelessness.

The Digiterati
In this knowledge-intensive age, support in cash and in kind from our new cyber-millionaires is crucial.

28.6.1998 The master-servant relationship is as old as the hills. Spartans had helots, Romans had slaves and medieval English lords had serfs and villeins. In today's more enlightened world where slavery has been abolished in most countries, a crueller and more universal master continues to drag his servants around in chains. His name is Poverty.

There's an old Yiddish saying: "If the rich could hire the poor to die for them, the poor would make a good living." Alas, the poor cannot even make that offer – death comes to all men. The rich can purchase longevity, but not eternity.

Poverty is a truly stubborn and robust master. Governments of every persuasion have spent the last century trying to dislodge him. Yet he still exercises mastery over two-thirds of the global population – four billion out of the six billion. Only two billion so far have escaped his thrall. Certainly in Britain and America, life for the average working-class man and woman is immeasurably better than it was in the eighteenth and nineteenth centuries. But for many folk living in Third World countries, life is just as hard as it ever was. Indeed, for many who are pressed cheek by jowl into shanty towns or who are eking out a living on land that over-cultivation is fast turning into a desert, life is even harsher. As Bob Dylan sang once, they live on desolation row.

So when I learn from *The Economist* that America now has 170 billionaires, 250 000 deca-millionaires and 4,8 million millionaires, and that the baby-boomers – on top of the money they've made for themselves – stand to inherit $10,4 trillion from their parents, a disquieting feeling creeps over me.

It also appears that the new rich – the digiterati – are not as philanthropic as the old rich. John D. Rockefeller by the end of his life had made donations of around $6 billion in today's money. All his life, he gave away 10 per cent of his income. The Silicon Valley tycoons are simply not in the same league of generosity. They lack the same breadth of vision. They prefer to support the expansion of libraries in the universities that the old rich established in the first place. Perhaps the new rich are not so worried about leaving a lasting legacy. The present is all-consuming.

One can even argue that the information age is serving to deepen the gulf between the haves and have-nots. If, as a child, you are given the tools to set off down the information highway, you're a "knower" and knowledge gives you mastery over your life. If you never get the chance, you're a "know-not" and ignorance condemns you to servitude. This new form of digital discrimination can only intensify the master-servant relationship.

It is therefore incumbent on the new generation of cyber-millionaires to heed the advice of *The Economist*. Namely, they should stop thinking that their wealth is entirely due to their own brilliance. Instead, they should admit that they owe much of it to the system that allowed and encouraged great wealth to be created in the first place. Freedom to succeed is a very precious commodity. It is the basis of the American dream. Unless the poor can dream, the rich won't sleep at night. And that applies as much in South Africa as it does in America.

Farming Equity
It would be a great step forward if farmers were willing to share the land with their workers.

10.5.1998 Towards the end of a presentation to the Bonsmara Cattle Breeders' Society of South Africa, I was asked a tough question. Did I think that land redistribution would raise its head again in the run-up to the next election?

My answer was one that the farmers were probably not expecting. To begin with, I had no more inside knowledge than anybody else in the room as to whether land ownership would be a major issue in the coming campaign or not. Presumably, some parties would have it on their wish list but maybe other issues like unemployment could overshadow it. Nevertheless, the present situation was untenable. So even if land didn't come up now, it would some time in the future. A constructive approach now might head off angry arguments and hasty decisions tomorrow.

In light of this, my proposal to farmers was as follows. Why not consider turning a farm into a company and granting shares in the company to all the people employed on the farm? After all, a farm is a business and most businesses have more than one shareholder. Obviously, the farmer can retain the majority of shares and therefore control. However, a crucial outcome of such a move will be that ownership is diffused. Hence, if any bureaucrat comes knocking on the door seeking to confiscate the farm, instead of the farmer saying, "Hands off *my* farm" the reaction from the entire workforce will be "Hands off *our* farm".

The shares can find their way into the workers' hands in various ways. My advice would be that they do not come free. Rather they're allocated immediately and the worker is debited with their cost. The debit is reduced each year by the dividends payable on the shares until it is totally paid off. However, the repayment may be accelerated by the worker putting up his own money. Thereafter the worker holds the shares in perpetuity and can pass them on to his heirs (as the farmer can to his). Any new workers (including heirs of employees who decide to work on the farm) will be subject to the same deal, i.e. they will be granted new shares in the business which once paid off they will own in perpetuity.

I know that some people will object to this approach on the grounds that it will lead to fragmentation of ownership (which is precisely what it is designed to do). Eventually, the farmer's family could lose outright control. But this is not necessarily the case if the farmer's heirs stay in the business because they will be getting new shares too. Moreover, if the number of shares allocated to a person is based on rank – which incidentally means that workers promoted during their lifetime obtain more shares as they ascend the ladder – then the farmer's family will continue to hold sway, providing their children come up to scratch as managers.

The most important change in mindset needed is that one is not dividing up a static amount of land into smaller pieces but an agricultural business into shares. Most farming land in itself has little value. It is the commercial use to which it is put that creates the value. With advances in technology, better working methods and the selection of high value added agricultural products, a farm becomes a growing business – literally and economically!

From an environmental point of view, the transformation of farms into companies is an eminently sensible idea. Given that South Africa is a semi-arid country, the land mass for the most part is quite unsuitable for subdivision into small holdings. Such a policy would wreck places like the Karoo by encouraging over-intensive farming. The majority of farms have to remain big. My proposal recognises that reality. At the same time, it would lead to a fairer redistribution of land than any scheme whereby a few black farmers replace a few white farmers, leaving rural workers and their families out in the cold.

Daddy Inc
We must use the family to create wealth.

24.5.1998 Here's a thought for the forthcoming job summit. Change the name to "enterprise summit" and concentrate on one of the most powerful business enterprises in the world today – the family.

Anybody who goes to London and visits a pharmacy or a newsagent will see the family at work. The quality of service has been transformed by an ever-widening network of predominantly Asian families. Shops are open for longer hours, they are better stocked and the assistants who are an assortment of the owner's older and younger relatives are not only more efficient but friendlier as well.

Accusations of child labour might be thrown at this arrangement when you see a son or daughter manning the till. But surely there is a difference between an alien employer hiring twelve-year-old workers and paying them slave wages on the one hand and children helping out their parents in the business on the other? One might even argue that one of the real downsides of modern living – working parents spending too much time away from their kids – is being avoided. Moreover, because the family has a purpose and is working as a team, it is less likely to be riven by disputes and even divorce.

I remember hearing a story a couple of years ago about a Durban man involved in the import-export business. He went out on a worldwide tender for new steak knives for the South African market. He settled on a Japanese company which, besides satisfying local demand in Japan, exported 32 million steak knives a year to the US. As part of the deal, he flew to Tokyo to see the business for himself.

He thought he was going to see a huge factory with an assembly line turning out millions of knives. Instead, he came across a network of small family businesses, each one specialising in one aspect of the knife. There were families who cast the stainless steel blanks, while others shaped them into blades and a third set of families sharpened the blades. Others made the handles and the copper pins which fastened the blades to the handles. Finally, the knives were put together by the business with which he'd signed the contract.

The network was serviced by a fleet of scooters which carried the components between their various phases of manufacture. Of course the scooters were owned by yet another family business! In this context, it's no accident that Taiwan has emerged relatively unscathed from the economic collapse in the Far East. The reason is that Taiwan most thoroughly practises the principle of promoting linkages between family businesses.

The great thing about running a business at home is that you can minimise overheads, you are not paying somebody else rent, you are not wasting time or incurring unnecessary costs on travel and you can choose the times you work. The summit should therefore explore financial incentives to induce families to set up businesses and ways of clustering family businesses together to act as a production chain like the steak-knife example. In addition, provinces and municipalities should examine the outsourcing of some of their activities to families, like street maintenance and rubbish disposal. For example, there are areas of India in which each three-kilometre stretch of highway is looked after by a family business. The state provides the equipment to make the bitumen and tar the road.

Thus, to eliminate poverty and create a full employment economy, the focus must now be on microeconomics and the family – and should move away from macroeconomics and grand solutions. As a bonus, this thinking will go a long way toward harnessing the well-entrenched culture of the extended family in our country and turning it to productive economic use.

40

BWKs

All our kids should read Siobhan O'Reagain's fantastic guide for K-TV Market Day. This was my preface.

6.6.1998 This book has been written for BWKs – business whizz kids. If you are thinking of becoming one then it is a treasure of good practical advice on how to identify and assess new business opportunities and then how to open up a business in order to take advantage of them.

The content of the book is very much in line with the seven principles that I recently identified for world-class companies in the book entitled *What it really takes to be World Class.* This is not surprising since big and small businesses alike have to aspire to being world class. The marketplace is so competitive nowadays that, should anybody be making an excessive profit out of a fairly mediocre product or service, other entrepreneurs will discover this treasure trove. They will step in, exploit the opportunity themselves and diminish profit margins all round.

The seven attributes of being world class are as follows: BWKs should think about them when establishing their first business.

✲ *Be very focused.* The most successful companies eat, sleep and breathe in very narrow niches. Don't try and sell all manner of things to the public. You only get ahead if you are highly focused and better than anybody else at what you are bringing to the market. Think about golfers like Tiger Woods and Ernie Els; cricketers like Hansie Cronje and Jonty Rhodes; or rugby players like Os du Randt and Joost van der Westhuizen. They all concentrate on one sport. Similarly, you should concentrate on one business.

✲ *Be different or unique in some way.* The best way to achieve this is to create a product or service that nobody else has thought about. However, there are other ways of giving yourself a distinct image in the market. Be especially courteous to customers because they like buying things from people who smile and to whom they can relate. Equally, think of what kind of experience you are trying to sell with your product or service. For example, Coca-Cola doesn't just sell brown liquid in a bottle. It sells the sunshine and youth that you've seen in all their advertisements. So you must brand your business in a unique way so that customers feel warm and enthusiastic about it.

* *Compare yourself with the best in the field that you are going to choose.* You have to think like a global player to be world class. Now you might say that your tiny business doesn't have to do this – but it does! Customers have so many options for disposing of their income. To attract them to buy from your particular business therefore requires outstanding quality and service. Look around at what your competitors are doing and do it better.

* *Have a perpetual spirit of innovation and continually seek to improve your business.* Life is not about taking giant leaps into the future. Instead, it is about taking a series of small incremental steps, each of which does a little to improve your business. The funny thing is that when you look back on how far you've climbed with these little steps, you will see how much your business has been transformed by them. Never rest on your laurels. Remember the fable of the tortoise and the hare. The tortoise won because the hare had too many rests!

* *Be flexible enough to realise when the market is changing and you have to adapt to it.* So many businesses fail because the owner has a fixed opinion of what is going to happen and the actual future branches off in a completely different direction. Be constantly on the lookout for changes in your market. They never happen slowly. They happen suddenly. So keep your radar system switched on all the time.

* *Attract talented young people to join you in your business.* You can often do things better as a team than as an individual. So be prepared to share part of your business with other talented BWKs. If all of you have a stake in the business and pool your

ideas, you may end up with something more original and therefore profitable than if you do it on your own.

* *Lastly, be socially and environmentally responsible.* Never rip off your customers, because they won't come back. Treat everybody who works for you fairly and don't pollute the environment. Customers want a warm, fuzzy feeling about the company they are buying their products and services from. An entrepreneur must be an upright and moral citizen in order to go far in the commercial world. You are only good *at* business if you are good *in* business.

Absorb these seven points, read this booklet very carefully and maybe one day you will graduate to being world class. Good luck!

Buy South Africa

South Africa is like a quoted company in a stock market called Africa.

10.3.1996 A regular reader of my column – "Worried from La Lucia" – has inquired whether we are on the "High Road" or "Low Road". In other words: will South Africa in the longer term – say twenty to thirty years hence – be a better or worse place to live in than today?

Scenario thinkers like me never give unconditional answers to a question like that. It's not that I want to be a fence-sitter. The truth is that the future has an irreducible element of uncertainty about it. The mist never clears. With our limited capacity for foresight, we dimly make out some possible pathways ahead. A few shadowy shapes give us some bearings. Signposts appear as the future becomes the present and the present becomes the past. But these signposts never offer complete evidence of which path we're on and often contradict one another. Doubt remains because the forces for good and evil are usually pretty evenly matched. The paths ahead at no time converge into a single certain road.

So it's all about intuition – weighing up the evidence at our disposal and placing bets on whether the future will go this way or that. Because individuals interpret the evidence differently, they will come to different conclusions. For this reason one has buyers and sellers in the stock market – both are groups of reasonable people who have come to diametrically opposite decisions. In the short term, one will be right and the other wrong, depending on which way share prices move. But in the longer term, who knows?

South Africa is like a quoted company in a stock market called Africa. Immigrants are buyers and emigrants sellers. For the last thirty years, Africa has generally been a bear market. On virtually every important parameter you care to name – income per head, education, health, quality of life, the environment – Africa has fared badly with only a few exceptions. South African émigrés like to dwell on this theme in order to justify their original decision to sell. Now, however, the time is ripe to pose two questions: has the market (i.e. the continent as a whole) bottomed out; and will South Africa outperform the market?

The answer to the first question has to be of the 50/50-variety. On the one hand, history does not guarantee that successive generations learn from the past. Progress is not assured. And there's always that old Arab saying: "Nothing can get so bad that it can't get worse." On the other hand, we are now seeing sensible economic policy-making sprouting up in many African countries that were previously sold on obsolete ideologies. In this global village of ours, the news of how to be a winning nation travels fast. Afro-optimism is beginning to replace Afro-pessimism.

Insofar as South Africa's prospects are concerned, I've always been a positive punter. My reasoning is simple: this country has the best chance of any in Africa of attracting foreign investment because of its modern infrastructure. And, given the changing sentiment towards Africa, foreign multinationals are not foolish enough to ignore a whole continent in their global plans. But one vital condition has to be fulfilled. Every ounce of energy on the part of the South African government must be devoted to creating a climate that is conducive for a new entrepreneurial class to grow and prosper. It's no good being lukewarm. We have to be like Thailand or Malaysia. Business must be an obsession.

This is not an impractical ideal. It does, however, require every community to pull its fingers out and do something about it (not just talk). Most of us want cream for ourselves as well as for our children. We want to be rewarded for the risks we take. Some countries overseas may appear as safe as gilt-edged bonds. South Africa is riskier but more exciting than them. Moreover, just remember one thing. Contrarians who buy at the bottom of the market reap the richest rewards.

Powell's Advice
Like a share, we'll be judged on our fundamentals in the long run.

3.11.1996 With the rand heading south once again, I think it might be useful to quote Michael Powell, who has established himself as one of the leading gurus of emerging markets. He was recently head of the Global Strategy Unit at ING/Barings and is now a private consultant. He makes the following points.

Cross-border flows of equity capital have sky-rocketed in recent years due on the one hand to the growth of large, global institutional investors eager to diversify their investments; and on the other hand to the growing dominance of multinational industrial enterprises keen to search out ever more profitable production sites around the world.

Most emerging stock market crises in recent years have started out as currency crises. These, in turn, were caused by short-term capital outflows. Consequently, investors need to distinguish between quantity and quality of capital flows. Every country needs a cushion of long-term net inflows.

High-quality capital inflows are likely to be positively correlated to underlying economic performance. Policy-makers should attempt to boost their economy's so-called fundamental surplus. This is defined as the sum of the current account balance plus all net inflows of foreign direct investment. Countries in surplus enjoy faster economic growth, firmer currencies and less volatile financial markets than those in deficit.

It is wrong for policy-makers to be too explicitly encouraging foreign portfolio flows because these are more likely to be volatile. Thus policies that favour the liberalisation of the financial sector over the deregulation of the real economy should be avoided. One must draw a distinction between an emerging economy and an emerging financial market. Portfolio investors ultimately get more satisfaction from emerging economies which over time deliver a sound track record.

In Latin America, recent reform has been skewed towards financial deregulation, but much greater real economic reform is demanded – particularly in addressing the problem of structural deficits. In sharp contrast, Eastern Europe is attracting sizeable high-quality, long-term flows of foreign money. In particular, inflows of foreign direct investment from multinational enterprises are swelling foreign exchange reserves. These countries now enjoy relatively freer real economies and relatively more regulated financial markets. As a result, they are better adapted to attracting the multinational factory than the often flaky and flighty mutual fund investment dollar.

Unless more radical free-market policies are adopted in Latin America, India and Africa, the emerging economies will diverge into a two-tier world. They will split into a virtuous circle of stable, fast-growing, capital-rich countries, and a vicious circle of volatile, slow-growing, capital-starved countries.

The relevance of Powell's remarks to the South African situation is clear. While our recent currency crisis is still modest by Mexican standards, it is testimony to our vulnerability to hot money flows. Whereas our highly sophisticated financial market is undoubtedly regarded by overseas investors as an important national asset, the jury is still out on the real economy and the will to implement programmes which will improve its performance. The rand will stabilise, or even strengthen, when the government is seen to be obsessed about creating a new entrepreneurial class. Support for the profit motive must grow from lukewarm to piping hot!

Volatile Stability

Sometimes the price of our share will be volatile.

9.11.1997 The polished black shoes are sharply in focus. Snapped by the owner – a potential suicide case – on the edge of a high ledge on a skyscraper. Cars look blurred in the street below. The caption reads: "The Big Crash: Asia's plunging financial markets send shocks around the world." The cover of *Time* was clever. The fate of the photographer is unknown!

Don't say you weren't warned. I wrote on page 98 of *The High Road: Where are we now?* the following passage: "So don't just presume that the Far East is a wonderful, well-oiled, economic machine that will purr along into the next century. There could be shocks."

But what are we to make of these turbulent times? Let me reiterate the paradox of volatile stability. The market is a global cop with a long and heavy truncheon which is occasionally swung extremely hard to punish governments that step out of line. As the currency or stock exchange of the erring countries goes into free fall, their rulers complain bitterly of conspiracy. Of course, the real irritant is that the market lies outside their control, something they're not used to. Grudgingly, they have to submit and restore good governance (or face isolation from the investment community). Any lapses bring further sharp blows to induce a return to the straight and narrow.

Nevertheless, the last few weeks represent a great buying opportunity because everybody – good, bad and ugly – gets dragged down when markets are interdependent and global, and information is instantaneous. Now's the time to separate the sheep from the goats in terms of both countries and companies. We're in a long boom of the world economy, the so-called fifth Kondratieff upswing, which will last through to 2020. Its underlying cause, as in the previous upswings, is the diffusion of exciting new technological waves. This time around, microelectronics, information technologies and biotechnology are powering the boom.

Moreover, we're experiencing a fundamental shift in values in all corners of the earth towards free enterprise. This trend can only help. But mark my words about being discriminating. We're in a falling price boom where, despite burgeoning demand, technology and intense global competition are driving down the price of virtually every commodity, manufactured product and service. Only world-class companies which are highly focused, in a perpetual state of innovation and strive to be unique in some way will survive. Only countries with world-class governments and civil services that provide a secure environment in which business prospers will bounce back in the near term.

The times are unprecedented for captains of industry and small entrepreneurs alike. It's a case of 1 or 0 like the binary system for computers. You can sell everything you produce if your unit cost is below the (dropping) global price and nothing if it is above. You either make a fortune or go bust. The gap between winners and losers is therefore bound to increase. Buying the stock exchange index on the grounds of cyclicality is therefore not a smart thing to do. Neither is it worth following chartists who extrapolate the future from the past. New rules apply and companies that can't cope are going to stay down forever. Rather be selective, based on the future fundamentals of the industry, or invest your money with professional fund managers with a track record of being selective. World-class performance will offer you a rising sawtooth pattern – long periods of good times interspersed with the odd correction but up overall.

Southern Rand
Sometimes our share price will just head south. But we should see that as an opportunity.

5.7.1998 Don't be too despondent. I'm talking about the rand. I know that in a previous column in this newspaper I argued for a steady currency. Foreigners don't want to invest in a country, make a handsome profit and then see it all evaporate in the devaluation of the recipient country's money. It is certainly not conducive to getting other foreigners to come in and make the same bet.

However, circumstances change and we should now see the decline in the rand as a positive opportunity. I know the viewpoint is doing the rounds that the lower the rand goes, the greater the number of young skilled people who will want to emigrate to countries of harder currencies. I know of the risks of imported inflation due to a sinking currency. I have read the Jingoistic headlines like "Raiders attack Rand" as though we're at war with the 25-year-old traders on Wall Street. Patriotism has its place but this is not the context in which it should be invoked.

Amongst all the gloom and doom, focus on this. Yes, foreign investors in South Africa have taken a knock. Some have bolted but many have stayed. Those remaining haven't lost as much money as the ones who invested in certain Far Eastern countries. All things considered, our investors have got off relatively lightly. Now the global investment community is looking for a floor to appear in the markets of emerging economies before re-investing. When they do so, it will be like a tidal wave. The Far East is no longer the flavour of the month, so we had better make sure that we are at the top of their priority list.

Moreover, the lower rand has provided much sought-after relief for our gold mining industry which is still a sizeable flywheel in our economy. But, that's not the real issue. Now is a heaven-sent opportunity to go for export-led economic growth while at the same time exploiting the high cost of imports for some substitution with local produce. With a pint of beer in the UK costing R20, tourism is the most obvious industry that can benefit from our cheaper currency. If I was a premier of a province, I would be going flat out to promote places like Durban, Cape Town and the Kruger Park as world-class destinations available at bargain-basement prices. I would aim my campaign particularly at the Japanese who must be feeling the pinch in dollars and pounds.

Nevertheless, I would do everything possible to ensure that tourists felt safe during their visit to my province. Security is such a basic need that unless it exists, no price will tempt people to come here. Tourism has a bigger multiplier effect on job creation than virtually any other industry. It will benefit big business and small business alike.

Now is also the time to establish a whole raft of other competitive export industries based on African branding and aimed at penetrating Western consumer markets. For example, clothes, jewellery, sculpture, art, furniture, wine, even mampoer, can figure in the drive. In addition, high-technology companies like Dimension Data can offer their services more cheaply to overseas clients.

A word of caution, though, about the current situation created by the cheap rand. It should not be used by the trade unions as a window of opportunity to crank up wage increases without commensurate improvements in productivity. If rand unit costs start escalating quickly again, we will end up in six months' time precisely where we were a year ago – namely a relatively high cost producer in world terms. We will lose the edge. So there has to be some pact to keep local inflation down as we lay the basis for an export-led recovery. In many ways, the currency speculators have done us a favour if we play our cards right.

Lessons from the Deep
We don't want to go the way of Barings or the Titanic.

12.3.1995 In my book *The Casino Model*, one of the chapters is entitled: "The global economy is a three-tiered casino". An excerpt reads: "The second floor of the casino has just been added. It is the "derivatives" market . . . The dangers of gambling on this second floor is illustrated by the magnitude of losses of some of the players . . . Without proper financial checks and controls in place, one trader in one transaction now has the ability to neutralise the annual profit made by 100 000 workers – or to double it."

I thought at the time I wrote this I might be being over-dramatic. However, the enormous losses suffered by Barings, the oldest merchant bank in Britain, and the indignity of being bailed out by a Dutch bank, underline the risks of dealing in the derivatives market.

That misfortune should befall such a venerable institution brings to mind the sinking of the *Titanic* in 1912. The City of London has up till now had the same infallible reputation as British engineering firms and shipyards enjoyed at the turn of the century. The products from both these sources – investment strategies now, ships then – appeared to represent British good sense and conservative craftsmanship at their very best. A few weeks ago, Barings would have been considered as unsinkable as the *Titanic* before it struck the iceberg.

Alas, neither the ship nor the bank applied scenario thinking which accepts that there is an inherent uncertainty about the future. They were both locked into the comfortable assumption that the future would turn out their way. There was no need for course corrections. Thereby, they placed themselves in grave peril.

The first principle of scenario thinking is to distinguish between what you can and cannot change so that you can adapt to the things you can't change and concentrate on improving the things you can. In the *Titanic*'s case, the designers never ran through the complete list of what they couldn't change, such as the freezing temperature of the North Atlantic making the hull brittle, and a glancing blow by an iceberg creating a shallow tear in the side of the boat (as opposed to a head-on collision holing the front). Yet the shipping line was woefully negligent about the things it could change, such as having regular safety drills among the passengers and a sufficient number of lifeboats on board.

In Baring's case, the bank couldn't change the rapid evolution of the derivatives market, which fulfills a genuine need for risk management by many companies. Furthermore, it couldn't change the advances in communication technology which permit enormous bets to be made by traders in a matter of minutes. What it could have changed – and didn't adequately – was its control systems and its procedures for screening and selecting staff.

The second principle of scenario thinking is to look out for seemingly insignificant and peripheral events which may become central to your future awfully quickly. The *Titanic*'s captain ignored several warnings given to him that icebergs were in the vicinity of his craft and sailed full-steam ahead. Likewise, Baring's management must have known that an unusual trading position was being built up in the Far East. The rest of the market did. But they misperceived its lethal potential. Correctly interpreting those early signs of impending danger is often the difference between life and death.

The third principle of scenario thinking is to keep opposites in mind as you make your way into the future. If anyone from the designers of the *Titanic*, to the shipping line, to the captain on its maiden voyage, to the passengers who only half-filled the first lifeboats to be lowered, to a nearby ship which mistook the *Titanic*'s distress flares for a celebration party, had played the scenario of "sinkability", a tragedy of such awesome proportions might have been averted. Neither was there a strong enough devil's advocate in Barings to play a disaster scenario. Its "iceberg" was a 28-year-old financial whizz kid, whose head over time was turned by a string of successful trades in the market. He eventually ran up a $27 billion position on behalf of the company. This turned sour, because the market always catches up with people who are over-confident.

My uncle used to be Chairman of Lazards, another merchant bank in London. I once asked him what he looked for most in individuals he was considering for senior posts in the bank. "Trustworthiness," was his response. He couldn't have been more correct.

Go Well with Shell

Rather we should be open to change, like one of the world's most profitable companies.

7.12.1997 Every year, *Fortune* publishes a list of the world's largest corporations – the Global 500 as it is called. Heading the latest list according to the measure of profit after tax is Royal Dutch Shell with a 1996 figure of $8,9 billion, up 29 per cent on the previous year. Second was another oil company, Exxon, at $7,5 billion, followed by General Electric at $7,3 billion.

But what captured my attention wasn't these stratospheric numbers so much as an article in the same edition entitled "Why is the world's most profitable company turning itself inside out?" Despite being No. 1 and despite giving its shareholders an average annual total return of 20 per cent since 1992, Shell is not resting on its laurels. It is following two of the principles I enunciate in my book *What it really takes to be World Class*: a spirit of innovation and the need to be flexible and open-minded about the future.

Shell is big by any standards, operating in 130 countries around the world and controlling every aspect of oil production from the well to the petrol pump. With headquarters in both London and The Hague, the company has a workforce of 101 000 employees, 54 refineries and 47 000 petrol stations. It is sitting on a cash mountain of $12,4 billion. So why the soul-searching?

The answer lies partly in the perceptions of the investment community. They are not interested in the past – they only want to know about the future and they're asking the all-important question: how, given its size and complexity, is Shell going to grow into the next century and where is it going to invest its enormous barrel of cash? The other concern is a reflection of the seventh attribute I nominate in the book for a world-class business – social and environmental responsibility. One of Shell's managing directors explained the fallout from the Brent Spar and Nigerian episodes as follows: "Previously, if you went to your golf club or church and said: 'I work for Shell,' you'd get a warm glow. In some parts of the world that changed a bit."

Hence, the company is transforming itself with the objective of becoming a fast, flexible, environmentally aware organisation. Management's vision is to be more efficient, more innovative and better able to identify profitable new businesses than at present. As *Fortune* says: "They've helped each other climb walls in the freezing Dutch rain. They've dug dirt at low-income housing projects and made videotapes of themselves walking around blindfolded. They've tracked their time to figure out where they're adding value. They've even taken Myers-Briggs personality tests to see who fits in at the new Shell and who doesn't."

One of the interesting results of the personality tests was that 86 per cent of the top 100 managers were "thinkers" – people who make decisions based on logic and objective analysis. In contrast, 60 per cent of the members who sit on the committee of managing directors (CMD) were "feelers" who make decisions based on values and subjective evaluation. As *Fortune* adds: "No wonder all those 'thinkers' had such a hard time understanding the emotion behind Nigeria and Brent Spar. And no wonder the CMD gets frustrated with the inability of the lower ranks to grasp the need for change."

The final word is left to Robert Sprague, Shell's exploration and production director, who made the comment: "We are moving forward briskly into the fog." His humour is self-deprecating but has a dash of realism about it. For the future, even with the best radar, is clouded with uncertainty.

M & G

So why not begin with some real lateral thinking on how to combat crime? Where I agree with the gun-free lobby in South Africa is that we should have much tighter laws on gun ownership, much more severe sentences for illegal gun ownership and a combination of frequent roadblocks and sweeps through urban areas to uncover illegal arm stockpiles.

22.2.1998 Congratulations to Meyer Kahn and George Fivaz for beginning to turn the corner on crime. Patient work in restructuring the SAPS and in establishing a crime intelligence network is paying off. Armed robberies have more than halved over the past two years.

Still, if the stated objective of making South Africa one of the safest countries in the world within the next three to five years is to be achieved, much remains to be done. Here are some further recommendations on law and order:

* Privatise, or civilianise, all nonpolicing functions within the police like equipment maintenance and station administration. Such pruning will allow the police to focus totally on their core business – the prevention of crime and the apprehension of criminals – and have more officers on active duty.

* Given the fact that we're still one of the relatively underpoliced nations in terms of cops per capita, we cannot in the short term implement the New York "zero tolerance" programme whereby every crime, great or small, is given equal importance. Prioritisation in our case is therefore critical, and a statistical database of where and when serious crimes are committed is the foundation of an effective allocation of our scarce resources. The SAPS should continue the good work in this regard.

* Distinguish between crimes committed with and without a gun. Suppose a man robs a supermarket and gets a basic five-year sentence. If it's proved he had a concealed gun in his pocket, he gets fifteen years. If he brandishes it, 25 years. If he discharges it without injuring anybody, 35 years; and if he injures someone, life. There should be no remission for good behaviour on the add-on part of the sentence.

* Privatise the construction and management of prisons. There are plenty of overseas firms who make a business of not letting prisoners escape. Award contracts for a fixed term so that on review the more competitive firms can bid for the less successful prisons.

* Allow more plea-bargaining in order to overcome the problem of minor criminals clogging up the judicial system. Give more sentences involving community work to those guilty of nonviolent crimes in order to make the prisons less congested.

* Outsource the prosecution of the more important criminal cases to private legal firms. Why should some of the best legal brains be confined to the role of defence?

* As we are not under imminent threat of invasion (the only significant enemy being the AIDS virus), assign appropriate parts of the SANDF to act as an auxiliary service to the police. For example, deploy soldiers on a 24-hour watch in key "hot spots" where car hijackings, muggings and armed robberies are frequent. Have them participate too in the protection of farmers and border patrols to capture illegal immigrants. Reshape the navy so that it mainly consists of small, fast craft capable of capturing smugglers and poachers of our fish. Turn the helicopter squadron of the air force into a rapid response unit capable of tracking vehicles used in security van heists and bank robberies.

C'mon, M and G, make my day!

Hijackers' Fable
The hijackers are still a constant scourge.

21.1.1996 There was a time when you parked your car in a city street in South Africa, and left your doors unlocked and your windows open because of the heat. You can still do that in Dubai and Singapore.

Then the downward trend started. Thieves stole the odd item of personal belongings from inside the odd car. So you locked the doors and closed the windows. You gingerly got into the car when you returned because of the boiling heat. But it was a minor inconvenience. For, with the windows open, the car cooled down after five minutes. Then thieves picked your locks. So you fitted an alarm to attract attention. But more often than not, it was ignored by passers-by. Then the thieves devised a system of smashing your side window, starting the car and driving it away in a matter of seconds. When you came back to your parking bay, your car was gone and you were very angry. So you fitted an immobiliser to the new model. But there again the thieves were cleverer than you and knew of ways of by-passing the immobiliser (or they simply put your car on a pick-up truck).

So you inserted a secret tracking device into the car in order for it to be traced if the thieves managed to get through the lock and the immobiliser. Then the thieves employed a scrambler to destroy the signal. Or they simply lay in wait for you outside your home, put a gun to your head and told you to switch off the immobiliser and the tracking device. They might even have taken you for a ride in the boot to make sure you did what they asked. So you went to your neighbours and said: "Let's build a wall around this neighbourhood and have restricted entry so that thieves cannot lie in wait for us around our houses." But the thieves clambered over the walls. So you added razor wire on top and asked the security firm which was guarding the gate to patrol the perimeter as well. Then the thieves grouped them-selves into larger gangs and sat at a safe distance outside the single exit from your suburb. As soon as you emerged some way, they grabbed you.

So the whole suburb pleaded for a substantial police presence in the vicinity. Many residents joined the police reserves; and the police, stretched to the limit, did as much as they could. Then the gangs merged and bought more sophisticated automatic weapons that completely outclassed the weaponry available to the police, the security firm and the residents. They had a habit of being at the entrance whenever the police were not because they had access to the police radio bands. So you mounted a public protest and demanded that the army should be permanently encamped around the suburb and armed convoys should be provided to the office, to schools, to hospitals and to the shops. Your request was granted. But, despite the convoys, sporadic attacks took place. Then you stayed at home in sheer terror.

Provisions of any kind were difficult to import into the suburb because the drivers of delivery vans did not want to run the gauntlet of being shot either. By this time, you and your family were completely under siege. So you decided to resettle on a high koppie way out of town, behind yet another wall. At least you could see the thieves in the valley below and could more easily hold them off. Luckily, the top of the koppie was fertile and, with the summer rains, you could grow enough food for everyone. You could even trap sufficient run-off water in reservoirs for the community's needs. Basically, your life had reverted to that lived in medieval monasteries and castles. The idea of going anywhere by car had completely disappeared. South Africa outside your fortress was a complete "no-go" area.

Half of this narrative – up to the point of putting walls around the suburb – is the actual past. The rest is a future scenario if the present game of cat and mouse between legitimate citizens and car thieves continues. Every move by one side prompts an escalating move by the other side. To retain a sane society, the game has to stop now.

Gangsters' Paradise
The press still underplays the atrocities committed by the criminals.

14.4.1996 A few weeks ago, I was at a business lunch sitting next to a senior bank executive. Her bank had been held up and some men had been arrested. In the trial, she had been called as a witness to identify the men. Never in her life, she said, had she been so humiliated as in the cross-examination by the defence. In attempting to destroy her credibility, they had succeeded in making her feel like a criminal herself. Moreover, she was compelled to give her name and home address in front of the men in the dock even though they were out on bail. The divulging of this information made her extremely scared of the consequences for her family. She vows she will never volunteer to be a witness again.

Last week, a teacher from a school in Alexandra Township visited one of our neighbours. She told their domestic worker that the latter's fifteen-year-old daughter who was a student at the school was pregnant. She had been date-raped. On a recent

TV programme, a schoolboy argued that girls could expect to be raped if they wore short dresses and flaunted themselves.

Last Monday, one of my wife's relations recounted how he had been the victim of a recent bank hold-up in Kinross. He had been made to lie on the floor for twenty minutes. The youth who made him do this put an AK47 to his head and repeatedly cocked the trigger. Then, by flicking the safety catch back on, he allowed the trigger to click without firing the bullet. A policeman who came to the front entrance of the bank during the course of the robbery did not appreciate what was going on until another youth, standing guard, removed a newspaper covering his AK47. When the policeman cried: "For God's sake, don't shoot," the youth replied: "I'm not going to shoot you. But see those two other guys across the road. They're going to shoot you." Luckily they didn't, but the robbers all got away.

At a dinner on Tuesday night to mark the retirement of one of Anglo's senior managers, the wife of one of our engineers recounted how she had been carjacked in Springs right outside her home three weeks previously. When the car wouldn't at first start on account of the immobiliser, the robber fired a shot at her at point-blank range. The bullet narrowly missed her. She managed to override the immobiliser and he calmly took the car.

And so it goes. Story after story. We live in a gangsters' paradise. It's no longer a friend of a friend who's had an unnerving experience. It's the person talking directly to you. The extent of the numbness the public feels was demonstrated by the way the newspapers in Gauteng reported on the murder of 98 people in KwaZulu-Natal during the Easter weekend. It was almost a byline. Even an article on the shoulder injury troubling golfer Bernhard Langer as he prepared for the US Masters tournament at Augusta this coming weekend was afforded more space. Our priorities must be confused when the murder of innocent families in their houses counts for less than a minor injury to a famous sportsman.

I keep thinking to myself that if 98 people had been murdered in Kent, England, last weekend this would have been massive news. It certainly would not have been business as usual. The

British government would have resigned and there would have been a general election fought on one issue only – the restoration of law and order. So how many hold-ups, rapes, assaults and murders does it take to have a similar impact on the national psyche here? Who is in control now – the government or the gangsters?

Springs Girls' High
We must look after our good state schools.

23.2.1997 I would like to quote a recent letter written by the Governing Body of Springs Girls' High School to the Executive Director of the Association of Professional Teachers. It was copied to me and to several newspapers. Bear in mind that SGHS is one of the best schools on the East Rand. From the desperate tone of the letter, one gathers that, unlike schools in richer neighbourhoods, SGHS will have difficulty raising the fees to cover the cost of additional teachers not paid for by the state.

"We, the Governing Body on behalf of the teachers of SGHS, wish to place on record our great concern and extreme dissatisfaction regarding the right-sizing of schools in Gauteng. This exercise has not only caused extensive trauma to the teachers concerned but is also causing severe problems for the remaining members of staff at the school, the pupils and their parents.

"We are of the opinion that should the proposed future pupil: teacher ratios be implemented, resulting in further reductions to our teaching staff, it will be impossible for our already overburdened teachers to provide our pupils with the standard of education to which they are entitled and on which we have always prided ourselves.

"Forcing a school of the calibre of SGHS to lower its standards so drastically can only result in a totally demoralised teaching staff and an inferior education which will be of no benefit to any pupil with aspirations of tertiary education or training. This school cannot survive any further cuts to the teaching staff and still provide quality education. Are we then to simply accept third world standards and allow an institution with a proud and proven academic record to fade away and die in the less than mediocre standards of the now not so new South Africa? Are completely professional teachers being forced to adopt utterly unprofessional attitudes and behaviour in order to be heard? It would be a very sad day if the teachers at this and other similar schools reached the conclusion that the only method to make the Minister of Education take heed of the exceptional dissatisfaction of the teaching fraternity, is to boycott classes and to mobilise a massive chalk down.

"Behaving in a professional manner no longer achieves the aims of education and therefore we request that the APT on behalf of all its members, take this dire message to Professor Sibusisu Bengu for his most urgent attention. The education of our children and the future of our country depends on the preservation of schools such as ours and the upliftment of all others. Please give us the opportunity to get on with doing what we are best qualified to do and what we most wish to do without unreasonable restrictions, while the education authorities concentrate on rectifying the problems elsewhere. This is the only way that a decent standard of education in this country can be achieved for all.

"Concentrating on rectifying the inequalities of the past is understandable, desirable and acceptable. Demoralising and antagonising an efficient, conscientious and dedicated workforce is not only very stupid but also shortsighted in the extreme sense of the word.

"This issue affects every pupil, parent and teacher throughout the country."

I've always said the number one characteristic of a "winning nation" is the quality of its education system. We're dead in the water in the global economic game if the good state schools decline. And it won't make the rest better. We're merely destroying the passport which allows a bright, disadvantaged kid to get out of desolation row. Abraham Lincoln offered wise advice in the middle of the last century: "You cannot strengthen the weak by weakening the strong." In other words, what we're doing now is nuts!

School Vouchers

And we need a system which puts pressure on bad schools to perform.

11.1.1998 In light of the disappointing matric results in many of the provinces, the time has come to consider radical innovations. But first it is worth highlighting the one thread that runs through all successful schools anywhere in the world: committed teachers. No matter what system is used – outcomes-based education, rote learning, religious schooling – the pupils will do well if the teachers are inspiring them.

Issues like private or public education, an emphasis on academic learning or sport, a competitive or co-operative environment, traditional or computer-based education techniques and the absence or presence of corporal punishment are trivial by comparison. As long as you have teachers who believe that what they are doing is best for the pupils and they're prepared to work long hours – well beyond the call of duty – to achieve their goals, success is more or less assured. Kids respond positively to enthusiasm, negatively to apathy.

And that's where the heart of South Africa's educational problem lies. It is not about resources. I doubt whether, if you doubled the state budget for education, you'd get better results. It is all about motivating the teaching body at each school. In an orchard, you have good apples, indifferent apples and rotten apples. You get paid more for the good ones than the indifferent ones and you get nothing for the rotten ones so you get rid of them. Next year you try to improve the quality of the crop. Precisely the same has to apply to the teaching profession. Good teachers should be given an additional bonus for their performance; the indifferent (work to rule) teachers should be induced to do better; and the rotten ones should be sacked (and that includes principals as well).

Two changes to the current system will propel it towards this outcome – more decentralisation and more competition. By more decentralisation, I mean school governing bodies not only having the right to hire and fire all teaching staff but also the right to fix the individual remuneration of each teacher according to performance. Accountability can only be achieved by beefing up the authority on site. Obviously a provincial inspectorate is still necessary to audit the way that school governing bodies are carrying out their duties.

As regards more competition, I would propose the idea of giving vouchers to parents to spend on the school of their choice – either state or private. The money would then follow the pupil: it would not go directly to the school. Good schools which attract more pupils would then improve their cash flow and expand their classes and teaching faculties. Bad schools would go bankrupt through lack of intake and be forced to close down. To give true freedom of choice, state-assisted transport for pupils on a daily or weekly basis would also have to be part of the deal.

This may well be anathema to many educationalists. But there's nothing worse than what we've got now with millions of kids being short-changed every term. If competition is the key driving force behind the improvement in quality of all the goods and services we purchase every day in the economy, why does this principle not apply to education as well? Why, if rich people can choose the school to which they wish to send their children, should poor people not have the same choice as well? The latter have as much concern for their children's future as the former. They also have the ability to tell a good school from a bad one.

OBE

Outcomes-based education will demand a shift in our educational paradigm.

13.9.1998 I was sitting in an empty boardroom at Wits Technikon talking to a box. The box was a television with a video camera on top of it and a microphone in front of it. It was linked to a similar box in Port Elizabeth with a roomful of people who were experts in education. They could see and hear me and vice versa. It was my first experience of being an active participant in a video-phone link-up.

What fun, even though the picture wasn't that clear. When

people moved, their faces tended to be smeared across the screen as if they were being photographed at slow exposure. Apparently, the movements will look less disjointed when larger packages of data can be sent down the telephone lines. Imagine talking to your girlfriend, boyfriend or mother-in-law by videophone in a few years' time when it's as common as cellulars are today. The upside is that you will see the person at the other end; the downside is that they will be able to gauge from your mannerisms whether you're telling a fib or not!

Even more fascinating was the content of the discussion: OBE, or outcomes-based education. The cyber-debate was arranged by Des Collier of the Delta Foundation. The principal speaker at the other end of the phone was Dr Bill Spady, an American who is the father of transformational OBE. He kicked off by explaining the difference between OBE and traditional educational methods. The latter use words like means, procedures, resources, processes, roles, teaching, programmes, curriculum, time, content, school. By contrast, OBE is about ends, purposes, results, outcomes, goals, learning, achievement, performance, standards, competence and life.

The reason for the name OBE is to move away from a focus on the curriculum as an end in itself to a focus on what is relevant to a successful outcome in the world at large. For example, it is all very well knowing every single king and queen of England since the year dot; you may have even remembered the dates of their reigns. However, other than winning a nod of approval from the teacher, you have to ask yourself how relevant this information is to getting through life. Equally, learning formulae for sines and cosines in trigonometry or how to differentiate and integrate in calculus may be necessary to pass Matric. Nevertheless, such knowledge has no relevance for most life-time occupations.

OBE, on the other hand, has as its objective the turning out of young people who have adequate maths for their lives and careers; who have communication skills and can express themselves creatively; who are focused on the future and have a working knowledge of computers and technology; who exhibit moral and civic responsibility and can work in a team; and who have an enterprising mind and a desire to learn new things continually during adulthood.

In OBE, exams are therefore seen as a culminating demonstration that you are competent to enter the wide world and make an effective contribution. Failure is not be construed as bad but a sign that the pupil hasn't yet acquired the requisite skills. OBE shifts the focus from those who can learn the most the fastest to giving everybody an honest opportunity to learn what it is imperative to know to make some form of living, and be a solid citizen. Furthermore, aptitude is defined as the rate at which we learn something new. Not only do different individuals have different rates at which their lights are switched on, they also possess different circuits so that their lights have to be switched on in different ways. That is food for thought from the point of view of not being too doctrinaire about educational methods. If it works, let it be.

Next week, I shall provide some of the answers that Spady gave to criticisms of OBE.

Spady's Defence
Despite numerous criticisms, OBE seems eminently suited for the creation of a new entrepreneurial class.

20.9.1998 I would like to report further on the enlightening conversation I had with Dr Billy Spady on outcomes-based education (OBE). He should know since he was central to its development in America.

One of the criticisms levelled at OBE is that allowing everyone to learn at his or her own rate leads to a large disparity of ages in the classroom. Spady responded that this feature cuts both ways. The smartest pupils will not be held back if they achieve the critical outcomes quicker than the rest. They will advance through the core system more rapidly, meanwhile taking additional courses in mathematics, science and other subjects which – though not essential for basic living – would open the door to professional occupations such as becoming an engineer, doctor, etc.

To a second criticism that OBE downplays the importance of

exams and thereby leads to a vaguer assessment of performance, Spady answered that the reverse was the case. Right now, most countries lack a proper definition of human competence and you can't assess what you haven't defined. Exams offer a very narrow definition of competence. Witness the number of students in South Africa who have been specially crammed for Matric and get plenty of "A" grades, only to fail dismally their first or second year university courses. They haven't been taught how to think. Witness the number of pupils in America who have fairly indifferent academic records but go on to become incredibly successful entrepreneurs.

Spady acknowledges that a certain level of haziness will always surround any attempt to judge a competent state of mind, but OBE tries to establish criteria as precisely as possible. Moreover, students are encouraged to assess themselves and their peers as well. In this latter regard, I was listening to one of our teachers on the radio the other day extolling the virtues of OBE. She had got the class to mark each other's essays, having given them the criteria to do so. She said that this led to a much better understanding of what a good essay entailed than having the teacher commenting on each and every essay and the pupil giving perfunctory attention to the comments.

My final exchange with Spady revolved around the ability of South Africa's educational system to adapt to OBE. Undoubtedly, the good schools in this country are already implementing the OBE philosophy, but what about those schools with underqualified teachers and a shortage of classrooms and textbooks? Will they meet the goals set in curriculum 2005? Spady and I both agreed that the worst approach is a bureaucratic one involving manuals with lots of techno-speak, jargon, rules and regulations. At this moment in time, the best thing to do is to give teachers plenty of room to manoeuvre but provide them with a simple guide clarifying the vision of OBE and giving a few practical hints and guidelines.

I liked Spady, I liked his directness and certainly this encounter shed light on a lot of misinformation that I had been fed on OBE. I hope I've done the same for you.

World AIDS Day

Don't make it just a day. We need a campaign all year round to fight the epidemic which, at the latest count, is blighting the lives of nearly three million South Africans.

8.12.1996 World AIDS Day has passed. It was dutifully recorded on the inner pages of our newspapers. I kept wondering how the press would have handled the day if most of the HIV victims in South Africa were white. After all, they splashed the one case of the Ebola virus right across their front pages. I'm not saying, for one moment, that they shouldn't have done that. It was a tragedy that Mrs Lahana died in carrying out her duties as a nurse.

Somehow, though, the contrast between the way the media have handled the impending AIDS holocaust and the single incident of Ebola suggests that black lives are cheaper than white. Another reason altogether could be that the public feel that any article on AIDS is crying wolf. After all, AIDS has been around for ten years and the corpses are not piling up in the morgues. "Where's the plague?" is the question asked by the man in the street. He concludes that all these doomsday scenarios are fanciful.

Nothing could be further from the truth. I have devoted eighteen charts to HIV/AIDS in *The High Road: Where are we now?* since it now represents the greatest threat to post-apartheid South Africa – besides violent crime. The percentage of HIV-positive adults in nearby Botswana has risen to 32 per cent. South Africa is conservatively estimated to hit that figure after 2010, but it could happen sooner. Nevertheless, the latest figure for life expectancy in 2010 for the average South African is forty (down from 63,4 years).

Imagine if we had an enemy on our border threatening to kill a third of our women in the second decade of the next century. We would resurrect the citizen force, purchase new tanks and military jets and declare a national emergency. However, because we're dealing with an invisible bug that kills you not immediately, but in ten years' time, it raises scant interest. This is also the reason for an absence of corpses. People are HIV-positive and healthy at the moment. The number of AIDS-sick only starts zooming after 2000. Even then they will die of TB and other opportunistic diseases. A cure and a vaccine may be around the corner – but don't count on it.

One of the myths that needs to be shattered is that the AIDS epidemic in South Africa is like the one in America. In South Africa, the main mode of transmission is heterosexual sex. Hence, whereas in America the preponderance of sufferers are homosexuals and intravenous drug users, in South Africa the victims are mainly women. An HIV-infected man is six times more likely to pass the virus to a non-HIV woman than the other way around. In other words, an unprotected sexual act is much riskier for a woman than a man. Yet the advertisements here still exhort men to wear condoms to protect themselves! Not a mention of the opposite sex.

Even worse, the number of full-blown AIDS cases among young girls 15 to 24 years old is appalling. This means that they became HIV-positive when they were 8 to 15. The level of child sex in this country would appear to put Belgium into the shade. But have you heard anyone speak of the rights of non-HIV young girls, and that having sex with them is not only a fundamental violation of their innocence but that it should be classified as murder as well? The silence from the legal fraternity and from the powerful women in this country is stunning.

HIV versus CD4

But medical knowledge about the virus is increasing all the time. They now have three-dimensional images of how an HIV virus locks on to a CD4 cell. It makes it easier for weaknesses in the structure of HIV to be identified and targeted.

29.1.1995 There has been a breakthrough of sorts in the battle against AIDS. It reinforces the notion that indeed a battle is being fought inside the body. What is surprising and new is the gigantic scale of the battle. Teams led by Dr David Ho at the Aaron Diamond AIDS Research Center in New York City and by Dr

George Shaw at the University of Alabama made the discovery.

In the journal *Nature* they describe how they were measuring the effectiveness of new drugs by counting the number of HIV viruses and CD4 lymphocyte cells existing in the body before and after a patient took the drugs. CD4 cells – also called T cells – are blood cells that form a key part of the body's immune system, its defence against disease. The results completely changed their understanding of what was going on.

Up till now, the fight between the two sides – HIV and CD4 – was thought to be a relatively quiet affair during the early phase of the infection. An almost dormant virus would make infrequent sorties against its enemy. However, by successfully entering the enemy's stronghold, it would use the machinery of CD4 cells to replicate itself and gradually build up its numbers. Thus the battle would widen to an ever larger number of fronts until finally the immune system was overwhelmed. Full-blown AIDS would set in and opportunistic diseases – like TB – would administer the final blow.

The research of Ho and Shaw has indicated another, even more dramatic, evolution of the infection. The drugs temporarily reduced the HIV population in the patients' blood by as much as 99,99 per cent. With a drop in viral load, the number of CD4 cells zoomed. The quick rise demonstrated that HIV patients were generating a billion CD4 cells a day. But the favourable situation was soon overturned. The virus aggressively replicated itself at about the same rate, fighting a pitched battle with the immune system. Furthermore, the daily billions being poured into the battle by the virus were cleverly altered copies of the original members of the force that had been 99,99 per cent wiped out. They were drug-resistant and eventually destroyed the benefits of the treatment.

Therefore, the scientists have concluded that under the macro-situation of the relatively slow progression from the HIV-positive state to AIDS proper, a series of microbattles of epic proportions between two fairly evenly matched contestants is taking place. Enormous losses are sustained on both sides, but the virus has a small edge. The handful of viral survivors from each battle are mutants which are genetically a fraction different from the billions slaughtered by the immune system. Like the stealth bomber, they have a surface which is undetectable by the roaming CD4 cells. They survive to multiply at a billion a day to become the dominant strain for the next battle. The CD4 cells heroically replenish their ranks too. Their radar system changes to detect the new strain and another pitched battle is fought. But in that new strain is another handful of clever mutants which ensure that the cycle repeats itself until finally the immune system is worn down.

This view of the progress of the infection also explains why at the outset the patient has temporary flulike symptoms. From day one, the virus is replicating at full tilt and it takes time for the immune system to build up its defences such that it can respond to the invader. As such, the findings point to a different medical strategy for combating AIDS. The virus should be attacked as early as possible in the course of infection with a cocktail of different drugs to wipe out as many mutants as possible. Then the resilient immune system can step in and cope. This is what is done with fast-mutating bacteria.

In South Africa, the most lethal threat to the country is not a visible, military one. It is the 800 trillion invisible microscopic HIV viruses that are being produced daily and spreading to other victims. Despite the breakthrough, one cannot rely on a medical solution to reverse this onslaught. Yet transmission of the virus can be stopped. It demands a different lifestyle. It is as simple – and as difficult – as that.

Triple Drug Therapy

Unfortunately, it now seems that the much vaunted triple drug therapy is less potent and more toxic than originally thought. Its cost anyway puts it out of reach of most of our sufferers. So our only defence is education, until a cheap vaccine or cure comes along.

28.7.1996 In 1992, I wrote the following about AIDS in the book *The New Century*: "The concept of combination therapy, using a cocktail of drugs to slow the disease and fight opportunistic infections, is gaining popularity. In countries able to afford a variety of treatments it may not be long before HIV infection becomes part of the growing class of chronic diseases. However, for most developing countries the cost of using combinations of therapeutic drugs will remain prohibitive."

It's early days yet, but doctors in America have recently come up with a three-drug cocktail which further research could reveal as a true breakthrough. Viruses, like HIV, need cells within which to replicate themselves. HIV belongs to a rare-ish class of viruses known as retroviruses. Instead of DNA, the genes of a retrovirus are made up of its chemical cousin, RNA. HIV's RNA has nine genes, each a blueprint for one or more of the types of proteins needed to make new viruses. These proteins assist the virus in binding to and penetrating the cell. They then persuade that cell to manufacture new proteins and new RNA using the genetic blueprints of the old RNA. An essential part of HIV's replication cycle is that it has to copy its RNA into DNA in order for the door into the host cell's nucleus to be opened. There the copied DNA integrates easily into the company of the host's genes, and by manipulating the proceedings of the nucleus causes the cell to churn out new HIV. The process of copying RNA into DNA is called "reverse transcription".

The objective of anti-HIV drugs is to jam a specific step in the replication cycle. Up till a few months ago, the two drugs AZT and 3TC were the front-line defence. Like a tag team in a wrestling ring, they were used to stop the specific step of reverse transcription. They won the first few bouts but inevitably, as their HIV opponent gained in experience and changed tactics, they lost the later bouts and finally the contest. The patient died.

But now a new class of drug has joined the attack. It is called a "protease inhibitor". Three products have been developed – Saquinavir from Hoffman-La Roche, Ritonavir from Abbott and Indinavir from Merck. A protease inhibitor interferes in a later part of the replication cycle – just when the HIV is exiting from the nucleus to assemble new copies of itself. The introduction of the new drug in combination with AZT and 3TC appears to keep

HIV permanently off balance: it is simply too confused to counterattack. As Dr Paul Volberding of San Francisco General Hospital puts it: "We have seen patients whose viral load has gone below our ability to find it." But then he adds: "The question is, can we keep it that low, and what will happen to the body with that kind of treatment?"

By themselves, the three medications can cause severe side effects; taken together the position could be worse. But the real problem right now is money: the annual cost of the three-drug cocktail per patient is around R50 000, putting it beyond the means of most HIV sufferers. For example, South Africa would have to spend more than 20 per cent of its GDP in the event that these drugs were universally dispensed.

This raises an important ethical issue. We all know that, generally speaking, rich people in the world have access to better medical care than poor people. Even where good state hospitals exist, private clinics can outperform them because they are under less pressure and have more money. Yet an abiding goal of the twentieth century has been to give people as long a life as possible irrespective of financial means. We accept that a richer person can have a better car or a better house, but there's something less acceptable about the rich being able to purchase more years of life. If additional tests demonstrate the efficacy of the new cocktail to the extent that it either becomes a chronic medication or – dare one say it – a cure, it's going to be mighty tough unless the drug companies lower their prices.

Road Safety

We must halt the carnage on our roads, which is the other big killer of our population.

3.12.1995 The article was at the top of the front page of *The Star* on 24 November. The five columns of prose were bracketed on either side by two heartbreaking photographs. On the left-hand side was a picture of a young boy and girl standing in front of a closed yellow curtain – he in a dinner jacket with stick-up collar and bow tie and she in a red dress. He managed a slight smile for the camera though his mouth was firmly closed. She was wide-eyed and radiant, her long blonde hair combed for a special occasion – possibly a matric dance. Their names were Charles Smith and Ezelle Els.

On the right-hand side was a picture of a young girl taken at her matric farewell dance. With brown hair swept back, her face exuded the kind of carefree happiness that we adults remember with nostalgia. Her name was Hester Booysen. The headline of the article was "Tragedy follows celebration as 3 matric pupils die in accident". All three, aged eighteen, were pupils at Hoërskool Monument in Krugersdorp on the West Rand. All three were travelling home at 11:15 pm after a fondue dinner to celebrate the end of their school careers. Their car crashed into a tree and all three of their lives were cruelly snuffed out.

As a father myself of a boy who has just completed matric, my heart goes out to the parents of the three children. It was the nightmare scenario come true, the one we all play as anxious parents when our kids go out in cars together. Charles's mother said what we would all say: "I wish I could have the last 48 hours back again." The words of Hester's mother also reverberate through one's mind: "And they were so nearly home when it happened."

In the same article, another car crash was reported, involving several matric students at Eden College in Johannesburg. In this one, Tammy Hatherell tragically died doing a U-turn outside the school. It's so difficult to know where to strike the right balance between giving our kids freedom and carrying out our parental duties of providing a secure environment in which they can grow up. How many of us lie awake at night waiting for our child to drive through the gates from a party and how many of us – particularly in these days of carjacking – become frantic if the appointed time passes and our kid is still not at home? How many of us phone around possible locations where our kid could be, knowing full well that when he or she walks through the door we'll get an earful about the embarrassment we caused? Some parents sigh with relief when their children move out of the home, on the basis that what they are not aware of they don't have to worry about.

I go back to my own experiences as a young driver in England. It was one of the great moments of my life to pass my driver's test and take my father's old Riley for a spin down country lanes and to parties in Sussex. I luxuriated in the independence that his car gave me. Soon I bought my own antique Morris for R500. The floor underneath the pedals had almost rusted away. It had to be poly-filled lest the driver's foot found itself in direct contact with the road when the brake was applied.

Students cannot be unduly restrained from driving on the road. Many of them will drive old bangers like I did. Many trips will be undertaken in a car packed with friends where the potential exists for the attention of the driver to be distracted by the fun and laughter inside. In order, therefore, to avoid more tragedies of the kind described in this article, we can only redouble our efforts to teach our children about road safety. Let not those four precious lives have been lost in vain.

The TRC

Apologise, forgive and reconcile. Now let's get on with the job of solving all our pressing problems.

1.3.1998 To say the least, I find the response so far to Desmond Tutu's recent call for whites to apologise for the past strange and disturbing. The general tone is anger, resentment and how dare you make such a call in light of the awful mess we're in. No remorse. No humble pie. Only aggression.

I guess people's memories are short. Not so long ago, opponents of the government were being murdered and we were paying the taxes to finance the hit squads to carry out their terrible work. Of course, people will argue that they didn't know that that was where their money was going. But we saw the results when Biko, Webster and other leaders of the struggle against apartheid had their lives abruptly terminated. How many of us stood up and protested and called for inquiries the way we do now when we

74

believe that government officials are being corrupt? Is corruption now more serious than murder then?

I think Leon Wessels' comment about whispering in the corridors when we should have been shouting from the rooftops just about sums it up. Complicity is not only about actively participating in dirty deeds. It is also about turning a blind eye to evil when you have suspicion that it is taking place around you. From a moral point of view, you have to step in and stop it. Otherwise you're as much of a sinner as the perpetrators. Basically, we were cowed into accepting cruel and unusual behaviour. We didn't do enough to resist it.

The TRC, I believe, has performed an invaluable role in exposing the depravity to which the country stooped in order vainly to keep the old order in place. The granting of amnesty, however painful for the families of victims, was a necessary part of the process. Without it, we would never have uncovered as much of the truth as we have in such a short time. It would have come out in dribs and drabs as the foot soldiers of apartheid confessed to their sins on their deathbeds to gain absolution.

In such circumstances, our past would have been a running sore that the nation would have constantly scratched to the point of bleeding. Reconciliation would have been impossible. Even now, many atrocities remain unexplained and will continue to cast a dark shadow over our society. But no process is perfect. At least we have some idea of what happened.

Yet, there is one other important consequence of the TRC which has been overlooked. Its proceedings and findings will make it exceedingly difficult for any future government to resort to the same type of dirty tricks in order to remain in office. The protection of human rights will be easier to maintain if we can point to the chapter and verse in our history when the minority systematically denied the majority these rights. The TRC has, in effect, drawn a line in the sand beyond which we are forbidden to step if we are to preserve our new democracy.

Never again can we suspend the normal rules of decent human behaviour in pursuit of some dubious notion like "separate development". Nor can we dehumanise those who oppose us in the name of "the total onslaught". The tragic outpourings at the TRC have been a catharsis for us all. But that's what Tutu is on about: redemption through the purging of the soul.

We, as whites, should count ourselves extremely lucky to have had such a peaceful transition. We owe it to our fellow black South Africans to apologise for the past and, thus released, get on with the business of building a better life for all – together.

The Sound of Silence
For a start, let's start socialising more with one another.

17.9.1995 "We must have lunch some time." This is a phrase often repeated in business and social circles in Johannesburg and elsewhere. The real and unspoken meaning varies from "I really don't mind if we never meet again in our lives" to "I wouldn't mind seeing you again, but the urge is not strong enough to make a specific obligation". Whatever the true intent, when we want to be, we're a pretty antisocial bunch underneath our polite exteriors.

The question is whether we're becoming more or less antisocial than our ancestors. At the brutal end of the social spectrum, we are probably no less warlike. More people have been killed in wars in this century than in any previous one. Issues over which people are prepared to shed blood still arise far too frequently. The pity is that weapons have evolved from those that kill people singly (clubs, swords) to those that kill people en masse (bombs, automatic rifles).

But it is the more gentle aspect of social interaction which I wish to focus on in this article – communication and human contact. For in this sphere I believe that we have sadly retrogressed in the last forty years or so. Simply put, many of us lead more lonely lives. We have lost the ability to socialise. Fewer of us have the sense of belonging to a community where people talk to one another on a daily basis, sympathise and help each other out. I wonder how many inhabitants of the major cities are permanently estranged from society, staying in their rooms or walking in the streets without sharing a single thought with anyone all day?

What has caused this decay? Many things. High walls and security gates have given us privacy, but they have locked us away from the outside world. No more sitting on the porch chatting to passers-by. We shop in hypermarkets and malls rather than gossip in the local corner store. Televisions, videos, CDs and computer games entertain us but they kill conversation. Families are more dispersed – no grandparents, aunts and uncles under the same roof with whom to swop daily experiences. More often than not no father either. Jobs are more remote from home. They demand long periods of silent commuting and make one too tired to talk at home. Factory workplaces are often too noisy to chat to one's colleagues. Office duties may offer little scope for interaction with other staff. Employees sit at their desks all day typing, adding figures, working – contrary to expectations twenty years ago – more days and longer hours. Or, quite the reverse, time hangs heavy for the unemployed with no sense of purpose and a great feeling of exclusion.

The irony is that in an era of material advances in telecommunication, we are actually communicating less with one another in a meaningful way. It's the twentieth century blues as individuals, lacking the sustenance of peer contact and sympathy, slip into despair. It's the age of fear and suspicion – don't talk to strangers, don't establish eye contact, don't give people a lift, don't trust anybody. It's the time when people relate more to the fictional characters in daily TV soap operas than to their real neighbours. As Simon and Garfunkel wrote: "No one dares disturb the sound of silence."

So how do we break out of the cocoon of self-consciousness that we're all wrapped up in? Well, next time, suggest a date for lunch and keep it.

The Mother City

In retrospect, rather than hosting the Olympic Games, it would be more sensible for this country to go flat out for the soccer World Cup. The matches could be spread evenly across the provinces. But the message to the Mother City about having a noble vision remains the same.

18.2.1996 A few years ago during a presentation I gave at the Nico Malan theatre, I described the impoverished communities surrounding Cape Town as a "ring of fire". I was criticised at the time for being over-dramatic. Nevertheless, whenever I drive out of Cape Town airport towards the centre of the city, I don't feel any reason for changing my opinion. The problem of poverty has been hidden behind fences; it has not been resolved. Residents of Bishopscourt, Constantia and other wealthy suburbs are deluding themselves if they think that somehow they are more secure than their "Gautie" counterparts. Apocalyptic scenarios can materialise in any area where a sense of relative deprivation persists alongside the perception that nothing is being done to improve the situation.

Why a repeat of the Nico sermon? Because Cape Town is in danger of looking a gift horse in the mouth. The tentative response so far from municipal ratepayers to Chris Ball's Cape Town 2004 Olympic Bid is understandable (they don't want the city mired in debt), but tragic. Baron Pierre de Coubertin, the 24-year-old French visionary who in 1887 conceived the idea of reviving the Olympic Games and saw his dream come true in Athens in April 1896, must be turning in his grave. More importantly, the wrath of Zeus, in whose honour the original games in Ancient Greece were held, will pour down on Capetonians if they continue to waver!

But let's look at a more earthly justification for being positive about hosting the Games. Every important city in the world has a distinct image which the majority of its residents are at least comfortable with if not proud of (otherwise they wouldn't live there). For example, New Yorkers like the idea of their city being the vibrant commercial hub of America, while Los Angelos prefer a laid-back, cosmopolitan atmosphere. New Orleans, on the other hand, is about jazz and Cajun culture.

So what does the Mother City want to be? Don't tell me the extent of her ambitions is to be the exclusive hideaway for reclusive millionaires. Nice to have them because of the boost they give to the local property market, but really there has to be more. The Olympic Games could provide an uplifting vision of the Cape of Good Hope becoming an African tourist attraction on a par with, say, the Pyramids in Egypt. They could also give inspiration to rich and poor alike to join hands in making the event a success. Wouldn't it be nice if whole communities got into the act of stopping crime because it was seen as an anti-social activity which could wreck the chances of the vision being realised?

Hence, I would suggest that ratepayers should quit worrying about whether their rates will increase. The additional cost of combating crime due to the higher level of unemployment that will result from losing the bid will completely outweigh whatever Capetonians will be asked to cough up towards the cost of hosting the Games. Anyway, Chris Ball has already made it plain that he is seeking as much money as possible from the national government for infrastructure including road and rail networks and sports facilities. He has good grounds for getting the money, seeing that although each Olympic Games is most closely associated with an individual city, sizeable benefits on a national scale accrue as well.

However, I have three provisos to the bid. Firstly, the Games here must be organised along the lines of the 1984 ones in Los Angeles which made a profit because they were treated as a commercial venture. Secondly, as much attention as possible must be given to creating sustainable entrepreneurial enterprises in the Western Cape, but particularly in the impoverished communities. Thirdly, the sports and village complexes for the competitors should be designed with the intention of converting them into assets that can be fully utilised by the general populace after the Games are over.

Let me finish by asking Capetonians one question: if an event with one of the largest television audiences in the world is offered to you on a plate, are you really going to turn it down? Please.

Clusters

However, the Cape Information Technology Initiative could have come to the right place at the right time.

23.8.1998 The Cape Information Technology Initiative (CITI) has produced a splendid little brochure on clustering. In it CITI defines a business cluster as a geographically bound concentration of similar, related or complementary businesses with active channels for business transactions, communications and dialogue.

Clusters share specialised infrastructures, labour markets and services. They are alive with networks and social ties. Everyone has a role to play. Clusters enable the businesses within them to achieve the results that wouldn't be possible in isolation. They act as magnets for customers, expertise, resources and capital. They spark innovation. They create spin-offs.

Harley Street in London is a medical cluster while Wall Street in New York is a financial cluster. According to CITI, Hollywood demonstrates the domino effect of clustering. Scriptwriters, producers, set designers, carpenters, make-up artists, stunt and catering crews, transport companies, the legal fraternity and a myriad of other film-related businesses support, help, challenge and co-operate with one another, ultimately building a flourishing and economically sound industry.

Another example produced by CITI is a small Californian valley which used to grow apricots until someone had the bright idea of transforming it into the most significant high technology centre in the world dubbed Silicon Valley. Then there's a place in Georgia, USA, called Dalton, where half of the world's carpet-making capacity is located within an 80 km radius of the town. Overall, in America, clusters employ 57 per cent of the nation's workforce and produce 78 per cent of its exports.

Across the Atlantic, CITI cites Northern Italy as home to a number of spectacularly successful small towns which in effect are clusters. Castel Goffredo has just 7 000 people but produces nearly half of Europe's hosiery. In Udine 800 furniture manufacturers produce half of Europe's chairs, and two-thirds of all imported tiles around the world come from Sassuolo's 180 ceramic factories. Modena is shared by Ferrari, Lamborghini and Maserati which must make it the sports car capital of the world. What these communities have in common is an active culture of trust, co-operation and civic mindedness – a culture which has turned Northern Italy into one of the wealthiest regions in Europe.

Birds of a feather flock together, so clustering is as old as civilisation. Athens and Rome were ancient clusters, as was Alexandria. As I've mentioned before, communities become world class because they're unique in some way. Many of them draw their uniqueness from the clustering effect – be it in industry (Detroit), art (Florence), entertainment (Nashville) and sport (Manchester).

CITI's idea of turning the Western Cape into the information technology gateway to Africa is both refreshing and challenging. In a sense the wine industry in the Western Cape is already a vibrant cluster. Of course, this was due more to nature than to human initiative. But there's always room for a second cluster. And IT, being knowledge-intensive, neatly fits in with the fact that the region has some of the best secondary and tertiary educational institutions in South Africa. They will just have to become more IT-orientated and develop the kind of research capabilities which can be used in partnership with the private sector. Good luck to CITI with its vision of grapes *and* chips for the Western Cape.

Eden

The Drakensberg is an appropriate place to reflect on the necessity for sustainable development.

1.2.1998 Down the valley to the right is a slate grey sky, occasionally lit up by sheet lightning so distant you can't hear a sound. To the left, the Monk's Cowl is just visible against the remains of a blue sky and scarlet-tinged clouds. Straight ahead are patches of dark green forest demarcating Van Heyningen's Pass as it rises up from the Injasuti Camp through a break in the

Drakensberg. Here I am sipping some Blanc de Blanc under a thorn tree, surveying this scene in the dusk. Quite a judicious moment to have thoughts on the approaching millennium, as the view has a perpetual quality about it, give or take a thousand years.

If one believes in the current estimate of the Earth's age of 4,5 billion years, then there have been four and a half million millennia since the Earth was formed. So what is so special about the forthcoming one? The answer is that it will be the People's Millennium – literally. Never before will we have entered a new millennium with six billion people living on the planet. At the outset of the one which started in 1000 AD, a few hundred million people at the most roamed the globe.

The figure suddenly started shooting up in the nineteenth century with the advent of modern medicine reducing infant mortality and prolonging adult life spans. We soared from one billion in 1850 to two billion in 1925 and then passed the three, four, five and six billion milestones in the last half century. We're gaining a billion inhabitants every ten years at the moment, though the percentage rate of growth is at last slowing down to the extent that the world's population may level off at ten billion.

Nevertheless, the pressure that man is putting on the Earth's resources is unprecedented and will continue to be so, whatever the future population trend. And yet, until very recently, we have never seriously perceived the Earth as finite in any way. Simply put, we haven't been obliged to. Our predecessors could basically do whatever they pleased without sparing a moment's thought for future generations. They indiscriminately cut down the forests for their farms, houses, furniture and ships and thereby altered the local habitat. But none of these activities could be said to have produced widespread environmental consequences of an enduring kind.

Now we're in a different world. We know for a fact that the recent forest fires in Indonesia have caused great aggravation in Malaysia and Singapore. Regional man-made smog is a new phenomenon. Meanwhile, we are familiar with risks like desertification, depletion of the ozone layer and global warming. All these problems stem from a vertical take-off in numbers of people who have to be carried by a static ecosystem. The air we breathe, the land we till and the water we drink have not increased one cubic metre in quantity since the advent of primitive man.

You may counter that advances in technology have promoted better usage of these elements within their ultimate boundaries of exploitation. You'd be right, and hence all the professional doomsters who forecast that we would run short of food, metals and oil by the turn of the century have been proved wrong. Indeed, the prices of both food and minerals have dropped by 40 per cent in real terms since 1960.

Nevertheless, Eden is getting more crowded. So I bet the next millennium will offer us a challenge on a completely different plane. Whereas we've grown accustomed to national rivalries and fighting wars with one another, the principal battle to come will be between material progress for the world as a whole and the limits imposed by nature. Hence, sustainable development is more than a green buzz word. It is central to our future.

The American Way

If unemployment is regarded as the number one problem in our country, the American way of solving it is best.

17.11.1996 A clear choice faces us now. Either we take the economic path to become a winning nation over the next three years or a failure of economic growth consigns us to hell. But what is the vision that will transform us into a winning nation?

Europe is emphatically the wrong model. Hardly any new jobs (net) have been created in Europe since 1960 and its unemployment rate has tripled. Because the business world is changing at a faster rate than at any other time in history, flexibility in the job market is essential. This is still not accepted in Europe, where lifetime employment with one company and regular hours in predictable patterns are considered the norm and entrenched by labour legislation. But what good is it to have security of employment with a company that's about to go bust? None!

If unemployment is regarded as the number one problem in this country, we should rather be imitating North America which has doubled its pool of jobs in the same period since 1960. Recent research has indicated that these are good jobs – not just ones of the hamburger-flipping kind. Americans have a completely different attitude to work to Europeans. They regard a job like acting in a play. You know that the play is going to come to an end some time. When the audiences start to dwindle and the box office takings begin to decline, you make plans to move on to another play. The average American has seven careers in his/her lifetime. The key word in America is "employability" rather than "employment". Acting experience and the ability to play a variety of roles – from comedy to tragedy – land you the next part. Interestingly, the largest employer in America is an employment agency (like Kelly Girl in South Africa), with 1,3 million people on its books.

The bottom line in South Africa is that the implementation of the new Labour Relations Act must be handled sensitively. If the consequence of the Act is that we fall into the trap of European inflexibility, then the already unacceptably high unemployment rate will simply increase further.

So what is the correct vision? Because we are now in a global market, we need to set our sights high. We must aim to become world class. But that means taking a leaf out of Rosabeth Moss Kanter's book of the same name. We have to develop and maintain three intangible assets:

* Concepts: the best and latest knowledge and ideas. After all, we are in the knowledge-intensive 1990s where the best returns are to be had in information and services;

* Competency: the ability to put those concepts into practice at best-in-the-world standards. This is where South Africa so spectacularly falls down. We have more conferences per square kilometre than any other nation on Earth, but we do not put our ideas into action. By contrast, the Americans are action-prone. They just do it;

* Connections: You have to be connected with the best nations in the world and copycat their best practices where they are of relevance to your own country. In this respect we have an incredible asset in Nelson Mandela, who happens to be the most popular head of state in the world and can therefore forge these connections.

These three "C"s should constantly be borne in mind. It may sound unthinkable for South Africa to become world class given the current shape of its economy, but one must recall how unthinkable the political transition was in the mid-1980s to see that the "world class" goal is an eminently sensible one to set ourselves today. Our mindset must change. We can do it.

The Zillionaires

In each generation, a handful of America's entrepreneurs become unimaginably rich. Incidentally, since this article was written, Bill Gates's fortune has risen from $12,9 billion to $51 billion – nearly a third of a trillion rands!

13.8.1995 "If I were a rich man." So sang Topol in *Fiddler on the Roof*. One has to distinguish, though, as my grandmother used to say, between the rich and the seriously rich. *Forbes* magazine lists the latter on an annual basis.

Topping the chart in 1995 is Bill Gates at $12,9 billion. He is the founder and head of Microsoft, which specialises in computer software. He was a Harvard University dropout whose MS-DOS and Windows systems now sit at the heart of 80 per cent of personal computers sold in the world today. In his latish thirties, he looks rather like the folk-singer John Denver with his tousled brown hair and horn-rimmed glasses. He certainly doesn't look like the world's richest man. But then one is beginning to see the ascendancy of a new generation of very hip, very successful, self-confident young entrepreneurs. Richard Branson, the owner of Virgin Airlines and Virgin Records, is the English (though poorer) equivalent of Gates. He cuts a somewhat more dashing and adventurous image than Gates with his exploits in hot-air ballooning and trans-Atlantic power-boating. But he started off more humbly than Gates in the business of selling second-hand records.

How much is Gates's $12,9 billion? In rands the amount is R47 billion. Now to put that figure in perspective, there are 47 million seconds in one and a half years and 47 billion seconds is 1 500 years. That's how much richer Gates is than someone worth R47 million. In other words, he's astronomically wealthy. As an individual, he is worth the total market capitalisation of Anglo American Corporation.

The world's richest man has always had a certain mystique. I remember when it was the recluse American, Howard Hughes. Hughes in his youth looked a bit like Errol Flynn in *Gone with the Wind*. He had a thin moustache and dapper centre parting of the hair that was so voguish in the 1930s among the smart set. He constructed an aeroplane with the largest wingspan in the world, called the "Spruce Goose". He flew it once over an extremely short distance and then locked it away in a hangar forever. He disappeared too. Stories surfaced of him as an old man with long hair and fingernails, and an obsession about being in a germ-free environment. Very late in life he made one final communication with the outside world to prove that a book written about him was a hoax.

Having said all that, I do not want to create the impression that super-rich people are necessarily unconventional. The remainder of the Forbes 1995 top ten include an American who is an ace picker of shares in the stock market and various businessmen who hail from Sweden, Japan, Switzerland, Taiwan, Canada, Hong Kong and South Korea.

Are they happier than more mortal folk? I doubt it, because the anxieties associated with looking after their vast personal empires counterbalance the additional freedom granted by a fortune in the bank. The law of diminishing returns comes into play pretty quickly after reaching a certain level of income and wealth. One need only study the lives of football pool and national lottery winners in Britain after receiving their windfalls. Most of them end up more miserable than they were before the event. They spend their time fighting off distant cousins who circle like vultures to pick up a share of the bonanza (an old saying in Britain is "Where there's a will, there's relatives"). You have to be accustomed to handling wealth.

We should not begrudge the Bill Gateses of this world their zillions. Unlike a lottery winner, they have earned that money by making a contribution to society that is valued very highly in economic terms. Each winning nation has its handful of entrepreneurs who satisfy the market on a cosmic scale. Let's hope we get a few more here in South Africa.

Agape and Eros

You have to hand it to the Americans for coming up with the discovery of the nineties – Viagra.

27.9.1998 To celebrate the arrival of the little blue pill on the shelves of our pharmacies, perhaps the advertising jingle should be Viva! Viagra! Viva! Trust the nation that gave us rock 'n roll in the fifties, put a man on the moon in the sixties, deposed a president in the seventies and introduced us to the personal computer in the eighties, to dream up the pill of the nineties. Americans have a knack for discovering a rich global vein and then tapping it.

I'm glad that the incredible popularity of Viagra has exposed how bogus those adverts and glossy magazines are which imply that sexual prowess is universal and anybody who has a problem is a wimp. As for those surveys highlighting the frequency of sex, you realise that either the conclusions were dreamed up by the authors, the only people who volunteered for interviews were the enthusiasts or the whole subject makes people lie through their teeth.

Whilst the discovery of Viagra is undoubtedly a good thing because it will solve genuine problems of impotency and release people from the emotional stress surrounding it, there is a danger of intensifying the myth that the source of joy lies in all things physical. The Greeks had two words for love – Agape (pronounced agapay) and Eros. Agape referred to religious or spiritual love, i.e. the kind of love that exists between an individual and God, a mother and child, sister and brother or between best friends. By contrast, Eros was the love between a man and a woman – erotic, sensual and physical.

Plato, the great Greek philosopher born in 428 BC, has also unwittingly lent his name to the type of love resembling Agape. After all, a Platonic relationship is one which involves the heart without sexual overtones. He would nonetheless have approved of this subsequent exploitation of his name. For he believed in a detached and superior world of ideas that co-existed with the actual world of material objects and experiences. The former was pure and eternal while the latter was shifting and offered only debased copies of the former.

He came up with a superb simile of a cave in which we are chained in such a way that we can only look in one direction at a wall. Between us and the wall there is nothing. Behind us is a fire casting not only our shadows on the wall but also the shadows of all other objects between us and the fire. Because we can never turn around and see the objects directly, we believe the flickering shadows are reality.

I think Plato's thesis has much to offer in today's world where sexual gratification or any kind of self-gratification for that matter is considered for real – an end in itself. Modern man is perpetually in search of the ultimate thrill, whether it's popping Ecstasy tablets, snowboarding in front of an avalanche, or bungee jumping from the highest bridge. "Take it to the limit" is an anthem for every age group.

But, as addicts of all kinds have found to their disappointment, each thrill only creates a restless and unquenchable desire to achieve an even more deep-seated thrill. They pierce a veil only to find another veil in front of them. The journey into hedonism is an illusion with only one ending – despair at never reaching heaven.

Thus, if the final years of the twentieth century spawn a new generation of Viagra addicts, the sum total of human happiness will not increase. Eros must go hand in hand with Agape, not replace it. Plato would have frowned upon mankind exchanging the constancy of love for the shadowlands of lust. Viagra has a special place in medicine. Don't let it become a cult.

Quiz Show
But don't believe everything you see on American television!

26.3.1995 A true 1950's story of mass deception has resurfaced as a movie called *Quiz Show*. It is directed by Robert Redford.

It is about a scandal which arose from the rigging of a popular television quiz show, *Twenty-One*, in the United States. The reigning champion, Herbie Stempel, was asked to accept defeat by the organisers of the show. He had to take a dive by purposely giving an incorrect answer to a relatively simple question. The organisers felt that, despite his immense knowledge, his appearance and background were responsible for a drop in the ratings of the show. "A face for radio" as one of them put it. He was replaced by Charles van Doren, a contestant with good looks, nice manners, a fair intelligence and an impeccable pedigree. To ensure that the newcomer would have a lengthy stay on the show, the organisers fed him the answers to the questions beforehand. So, the new contestant mopped his brow in his soundproof booth, feigned intense concentration and delivered his lines perfectly. He became a national hero and appeared on the cover of *Time* magazine.

When the scam was uncovered, the organisers tried to justify their action by saying that the quiz show was first and foremost entertainment. If the whole thing was staged, so what? The public enjoyed the drama – real or manipulated. Of course, the organisers were.wrong. The public were seriously taken aback by the revelation. They perceived a major difference between a genuine contest and an artificial show-business lookalike. Thenceforward, they never again had the same unqualified faith in the material served up on American television.

Examples of mass deception of varying degrees of dishonesty still abound on the box. Docu-dramas purport to give the inside track on real incidents and real lives. In actual fact, they often reflect the director's perceptions and prejudices. The truth is modified to fit the message. Elsewhere, debates among experts on air may be rehearsed in advance, the cut and thrust not quite being so spontaneous as it seems. Moreover, those "live" talk shows featuring prominent personalities may have been taped and edited to remove fluffs and embarrassing moments.

Illusion blends more subtly with reality in news programmes. It's not so much that an individual item is in any way misleading. It's the choice between what is inserted and what is omitted that leads to a distorted image. The items shown have to be spectacular enough to hold the public's attention. Otherwise, they may switch to another channel.

Hollywood has always been a place for legitimate deception. But special effects are getting better all the time. A sweeping landscape or a city street may now be purely an image created by computers in a digital studio. The actors play their parts against a blank blue screen. A day will come when "virtual stars" can be simulated for entire movies by clever computer artists and technicians. Such stars will be totally lifelike but no more real than the cartoon characters we have now. They have already learnt how to paste an actor's digitised image into the unfinished bits of a film. This was done for Brandon Lee who died on location during the shooting of *The Crow*.

In art, mass deception is as old as the hills. How many masterpieces are hanging in national galleries that are really fakes? It may be a beautiful picture in itself, but something is definitely missing if the master didn't actually do it himself. In literature, how many ghostwriters have stood in for the famous names on the cover? In music, Milli Vanilli was discovered to be lip-synching the recorded voices of other singers because they could not sing themselves. In the material world, is that Hermes scarf, Rolex watch or Gucci handbag you're looking at the real thing or just a rip-off from the Far East?

I guess the biggest disappointment for me is mass deception in sport: athletes who break world records on steroids, "shamateurism" in rugby and now the possibility of soccer and cricket matches where the results have been bent. It started with the odd horse race and wrestling bout. Where is it all going to end?

Disraeli once said: "There are three kinds of lies. Lies, damned lies and statistics." To these we can add a fourth category – the most dangerous of all because its roots are in money – "true lies".

Brands of Democracy
I've always liked a political system where there is plenty of cut and thrust and MPs have to stay in touch with their constituencies.

20.11.1994 The recent landslide election victory for the Republican Party in the United States, giving them control of both the

Senate and the House of Representatives, has already been subjected to thorough analysis. Pundits put it down to reasons varying from President Clinton's aimlessness to a shift towards more conservative values among the American public to frustration with the lavish plans for health-care reform.

The angle I wish to come from is completely different. For me, the election results were a celebration of the American brand of democracy, where major swings and upsets are possible. The South African brand of democracy in its transitional form, though resembling the American brand in certain important respects, differs in some critical ways too. Let's examine the similarities and differences.

Both brands have one person, one vote. Both brands have a national poll for president, though in South Africa the leader of the party winning the national election becomes president whereas in the US it is a run-off between individuals. Both brands have a form of dual balloting where separate votes are cast for representatives in the national parliament on the one hand and representatives in the regional/state parliaments on the other.

That is about where the common features end. The US is divided up into constituencies for the purposes of electing both national and state representatives. Each national and each state representative is accountable to the constituency which elects him or her. South Africa at the moment has national and regional lists of representatives chosen by the parties themselves. They are not accountable to specific constituencies. Secondly, the US has for each constituency a simple first-past-the-post principle where the candidate securing the majority of votes wins. In South Africa, we have proportional representation where the seats in the national and regional parliaments are allocated according to the share that each party has of the total vote.

Thirdly, the US has elections every two years for the whole of the House of Representatives and for one-third of the Senate (each senator having a six-year term). The US president is elected to serve for four years. The net result is that the popularity of the policies of the opposing parties is put to the test every two years.

In South Africa, the length of the term of office of future national and regional parliaments still has to be settled, although five years is often spoken of as a reasonable figure.

When weighing up the pros and the cons of the American brand of democracy versus the South African transitional brand, I have to express a preference for the American one. It is only through a constituency system that each politician has a personal link to a community small enough for each to get to know the other. There is a human touch between them. It is only through election results being based on simple majorities that an inefficient and corrupt administration can be completely swept out and replaced by another party. It is only through holding elections reasonably frequently that one keeps politicians on their toes and aware of swings in public opinion.

I know the arguments against this type of democracy only too well. Constituency-based politics can deteriorate into "pork barrel" politics, where each representative puts local issues above national interests. Simple majoritarianism produces a less representative parliament than proportional representation and penalises smaller parties. Too short a term of office makes representatives pander to popular whims and fancies and conversely lessens their willingness to make unpopular but wise decisions. Moreover, it is overly costly to hold elections too frequently.

Nevertheless, it is interesting that the American brand of democracy has endured virtually unchanged. Meanwhile, the Italian and the Japanese brands, based as they have been on proportional representation, are being adapted to fall more into line with simple first-past-the-post principles. It seems that it is becoming more generally accepted that the most important check on a government's power is an effective political opposition waiting in the wings; and the best way of achieving the latter is the American way. We do not have – indeed have not had in the last 46 years – a genuine alternative government-in-waiting opposition party in South African politics. Will we ever?

California Dreamin'

Sometimes America makes a lousy political decision; but the courts have since stepped in to reverse this one.

1.1.1995 "We're all goin' on a surfin' safari", "California dreamin' on such a winter's day", "I wish they all could be California Girls", "If you're goin' to San Francisco, be sure to wear some flowers in your hair . . ."

Snatches of songs from the sixties when California was the hippest, coolest place in the world to be. And since then it hasn't been just music either. Palo Alto has had Tom Peters, the Billy Graham equivalent of management gurus. Silicon Valley has had the geniuses who concentrate the power of room-sized fifties' computers onto a chip the size of a thumbnail.

And now Proposition 187, which is not just conservative, but goes against the grain of what California epitomised to us as teenagers – the brotherhood of man. The proposition bans illegal immigrants from access to all public services except emergency health-care. It was supported by 59 per cent of those who voted in the mid-term Californian elections. The carefree Californian baby-boomers have grown up. They have developed the normal middle-aged anxieties about state budget deficits, security for their families, keeping their jobs and so on. They are enraged with squatters on their doorstep.

The proposition means that if a child's parents managed to smuggle him illegally across the Rio Grande to give him a better life in California away from the harsh, unrelenting poverty of some South American slum, the doors from now on will be slammed in his face. If he wants to go to school, he must show a pass he does not possess. If he's got a pain in his stomach and it's not appendicitis, he must leave the hospital. If anything is de-signed to create a subterranean, second-class noncitizenry, this is it. Like Prohibition in the twenties, it is a golden opportunity for gangsters to come in and exploit the situation. They will peddle forged documents and provide "protection" for large sums of money.

In 1991, I published a book entitled *The New Century: Quest for the High Road*. In the book, the "High Road/Low Road" scenarios were generalised to cover the world as a whole. In the "High Road" the rich nations transfer technology and open up markets to the poor nations, creating in the process an all-inclusive global economy. Governments of the poor countries respond by adopting political and economic formulas for turning themselves into "winning nations". Synergy between the "rich old millions" and "poor young billions" leads to a better world in the next century.

The "Low Road" is where the "rich old millions" retire into a gilded cage, protecting their own markets to the exclusion of the rest of the world. They try to stop their own countries from being swamped by billions of refugees on the other side of the cage by ever-tougher anti-immigration measures. The attempt fails. The gap between rich and poor widens. The refugees find a way in. Armies cannot repel them.

California, by voting in favour of this short-sighted measure, is making the wrong choice. However, it is not out of line. Countries in Europe have already tightened up and Japan has always been strict about immigrants. Unfortunately, it is the natural tendency of the haves – when they feel threatened – to build high walls as security against the have-nots. Yet, there's a simple truth. You only have real security if people outside your walls are so preoccupied and busy with their own lives that they are not interested in climbing your walls. Until the US (with the assistance of Canada) provides the leadership which helps Central and South American countries to attain their own versions of the "High Road", people will not quit moving from south to north. They have nothing to lose.

For South Africa, the only difference is the points of the compass. Unless we help to stabilise the region around us by creating a Southern African Common Market, the refugees will continue to flow in from the north, the west and the east. Electric fences will prove as futile in the long run as Proposition 187.

Lessons of Watergate
Occasionally America demonstrates that no one is above the law.

19.2.1995 Unorthodox means of trying to win an election were part and parcel of the original "Watergate". They brought down an American president: Richard Nixon. In retrospect, he never had to cheat to win. The election was his for the taking. For those who are too young to remember, "Watergate" was divided into two parts – the original felony of breaking and entering the offices of a political competitor and the cover-up of the felony.

Before and after the downfall of Nixon, this pattern has been repeated over and over again in many countries. Petty officials commit a crime, then an important political figure steps in to deny any wrongdoing and tries to cover up for the petty officials. Often noble causes or extraordinary circumstances are shamelessly cited as a justification for the action. The press is not put off. It senses blood and unleashes its best investigative journalists to strip away the deception layer by layer until the truth is exposed.

The common thread is that, as each stage of these sagas sadly unfolds, it's the cover-up that becomes the focus of attention. In the minds of the public, this seriously compounds the immorality of the act. As higher levels of complicity are revealed, the thrill of the chase is on. Satisfaction is only achieved when the quarry at the top is hunted down, cornered and shredded. Hence, where a political leader has had no prior information of a crime being committed by his followers and is therefore innocent of the deed itself (though possibly guilty of dereliction of duty), he has only one course to follow. Once he has been apprised of the situation, he should publicly acknowledge the transgression and speedily take disciplinary action against those involved. He might then emerge from the affair unscathed.

What will undoubtedly jeopardise the position of a leader is the withholding of details of an impropriety from the public domain whilst he is "in the know". By that fact alone, his integrity is compromised and he can be considered an accessory. He can no longer distance himself from the perpetrators. He can even be blackmailed by them, because they know he knows and they know that he has much more to lose than they do by the spilling of the beans. The longer the matter does not surface, the more powerful the accusation of non-disclosure becomes. Thus conspiracies of silence are born to save skins all around.

Transparency – the opposite of cover-up – really does serve a purpose. It protects political leaders from the errors and misdemeanours of subordinates who are busy lining their own pockets or mistakenly think that their actions are in the party's or in the national interest. Transparency pre-empts the leader from ever being placed in the invidious position of having to choose between protecting political colleagues for their long-serving loyalties and destroying them publicly for unreasonable conduct. If they are perceived to have done wrong, transparency demands that they be suspended from office, arrested, brought to trial and judged in a court of law. Personal relationships are simply irrelevant if one believes that everybody is subject to the law of the land. Guilt or innocence – as determined by the court – is the ultimate arbiter of an individual's fate.

As South Africa seeks to transform itself into a just, equitable society, people would do well to ponder this. If you relax on corruption, it will spread unbelievably fast. Every aspect of life will be subject to a bribe being given or taken. Moreover, the genie can never be put back into the bottle. Those who have the money and are prepared to be unscrupulous will have suitable doors opened for them and fulfill their ambitions. Those who are honest or who don't have the money will lead lives perpetually stunted by a bureaucracy whose palms they will not or cannot cross. Is that justice? Is that equality? No!

Assassins
On the other hand, the number of guns in private hands in America means that no public figure is safe.

19.11.1995 Just as gravitation keeps binary stars eternally circling one another in the cosmos, an assassination inextricably links the names of the killers and the killed for the rest of time. Generations of schoolchildren have learnt that on the Ides of March in 44 BC, Gaius Cassius and Marcus Brutus were among the group who slew Julius Caesar as he entered a senate meeting. They may also know that in 1865 John Wilkes Booth accounted for Abraham Lincoln, while he sat in Ford's Theatre in Washington DC just days after the Union victory.

In modern times, the most renowned assassination was that of John Kennedy at 12:30 pm on 22 November 1963 by Lee Harvey Oswald as the President and his wife, Jacqueline, were riding slowly through downtown Dallas in an open limousine. Two bullets from Oswald's rifle struck Kennedy at the base of his neck and in the head. He was dead upon arrival at Parkland Memorial Hospital. I remember hearing the news while I walked across the chilly quadrangle of New College, Oxford. Two days later Oswald was to die in the basement of a Dallas police station, shot at point-blank range by Jack Ruby.

Then on 4 April 1968, the dream of one of America's most charismatic civil rights leaders was rudely cut short by a sniper. Martin Luther King was standing on the balcony of a motel in Memphis when he was murdered by James Earl Ray. In the same year, just after midnight on 4 June, Bobby Kennedy was walking through the kitchen hallway of the Ambassador Hotel in Los Angeles. He was campaigning for the Democratic Party candidacy for presidency. He was gunned down by Sirhan Bishara Sirhan. Who can forget the photograph of Bobby lying stricken on the floor, his legs akimbo, his eyes staring glassily at the ceiling?

In 1980, a nonpolitical assassination occurred that devastated millions of music lovers. John Lennon, who wrote "Give peace a chance", was killed outside his apartment building in New York City by Mark Chapman.

Now we have the terrible assassination of Yitzhak Rabin by Yigal Amir on 4 November 1995, as the Israeli Prime Minister was leaving a peace rally in Tel Aviv. The picture that will remain in my mind is that of Rabin's longtime aide, Eitan Haber, speaking at the funeral. He held aloft Rabin's bloodstained copy of the "Song of peace" with a bullet hole through it as he said:

"Yitzhak, you know you had a thousand merits, but singing was not your strength. You sang off key. Then, as always, you folded the paper in four parts and, as always, put it in your jacket pocket."

Down the centuries, real assassins seldom accord with the fictional stereotypes found in movies and books. For example, the film *Assassins*, currently on the South African circuit, is the story of rivalry between two professional killers who dispatch victims with cool detachment and consummate skill. Real assassins, on the other hand, are usually passionate oddballs stalking a single quarry for a deranged motive. Cassius and Brutus were disgruntled Republicans who did not wish to see Caesar become king. Booth was a Confederate fanatic. Oswald was an ex-Marine and Marxist sympathiser. Ruby was a nightclub owner who wanted to be a national hero by being an assassin's assassin. Sirhan was a Palestinian zealot, Ray a released convict and Chapman a crazed fan. As for Amir, a conservative law student, he asserted that it was a crime punishable by death to hand over land to the enemy.

Many real assassins are successful because their potential for harm is not suspected beforehand and they are prepared to be arrested afterwards. As Amir's mother, a kindergarten teacher in a middle-class Tel Aviv suburb, recalled: "I was shocked when police found enough explosives at our home to blow it all sky-high. I have been criticised for not realising that he had weapons and ammunition in the house. But, as any mother will know, if a child wants to hide something he will know how to do it. When I went upstairs, I asked the police 'What are those bars of soap?' When they explained it to me, it took perhaps an hour or two to digest what he left up there." That was Amir's lethal quality. He was an unknown quantity – even to his parents.

Abortion

It's amazing how divided America is on this issue. We seem to have satisfactorily resolved it here.

14.7.1996 It is said in America that if the media want to ensure that any presidential hopeful loses half his support, they ask him one question on camera: "Are you pro-abortion or pro-life?" If the hopeful says he's pro-abortion, he immediately loses his conservative and deeply religious voters. If he says he's pro-life, out of the window goes the left wing and much of the female vote. If, seeing the abyss on both sides, he qualifies his answer to the extent that he meets himself coming the other way, he is judged indecisive and still loses half his supporters who want a strong and forthright leader. So it's a no-win situation.

Bob Dole has recently gone through this torment. The pragmatic section of the Republican Party have bluntly said that he can't win the presidency by sticking to a straight anti-abortion platform. The conservatives have said that they'll dump him if he shows any shred of a moral climb-down. So he's opted for the fudge by saying that he would like to see a "declaration of tolerance" in the party manifesto and he wouldn't mind a running mate who did not share his anti-abortion views. It will be interesting to see if this strategy works.

America feels so strongly about this issue that there have been examples of doctors who perform abortions being gunned down and clinics being set alight. And now South Africa has opened the hornet's nest with its abortion-on-demand bill. It has already drawn the retort from the religious lobby that it is strange to have policy-makers who are not prepared to execute convicted murderers but who are prepared to terminate the life of innocent, unborn children.

Van Zyl Slabbert made a profound statement in a speech I was listening to the other day about how difficult it is to govern a modern country. He observed: "It's easy to choose between good and bad. The hardest choices – and inevitably most of them are this way now – are between good and good." That point fits the abortion debate perfectly, for you have two "goods" directly counterpoised – the right to life on the one hand and the right of a woman to make her own choice about her own body on the other.

At Oxford, I was the only candidate in my college who in his final year chose to specialise in philosophy as part of the politics, philosophy and economics degree. I therefore had the privilege of having solo weekly tutorials with one of Oxford's finest philosophers of the time – Anthony Quinton. To indicate the difficulties in philosophy, he delighted in posing examples which were irresolvable through normal logical means.

Applying his technique to abortion, let's pose the example of a fourteen-year-old girl who is gang-raped by complete strangers and wants to have an abortion. Do you deny her the choice and possibly condemn her to a lifetime of pain, either looking after a kid that she didn't want or feeling guilty about giving up the kid for adoption? Or do you grant her the choice, which means that a soul that is now on the assembly line never gets the chance of existence outside the womb?

Of course, the middle-of-the-roader will answer that a number of weeks must elapse before a foetus has a soul. If you intervene before then, nobody gets killed because nobody exists. You are therefore not breaking the commandment "Thou shalt not kill". But this is specious stuff, because the inevitable rebuttal is: take any number of weeks you like, what is the divine significance of that number such that less than the number there's no soul, more than the number there is. Where is there any scientific evidence that a soul suddenly becomes the property of a foetus other than when it comes into being, i.e. at conception?

So there's no easy answer. It all depends on whether or not you think the right of the girl to choose overrides the right of the foetus to life. The drafters of the new bill have decided in favour of the girl.

Euthanasia
Now, with the geriatric boom and doctors making inheritance an
obsolete concept, this is becoming a hot issue too.

8.1.1995 According to a British magazine which recently conducted a poll among 2 500 elderly readers, nine out of ten old
people living in Britain support euthanasia. In other words, they
believe that doctors should be allowed to end the lives of
terminally ill patients who want to die. They would also like a
relative to ask a doctor to end their life if they are too ill to com-
municate.

In February 1994, however, a Select Committee on Medical
Ethics – consisting of peers from the House of Lords – said that
Britain should keep its ban on euthanasia. They were asked to
examine the issue in early 1993 subsequent to a British doctor
being found guilty of attempted murder for giving a lethal dose
of drugs to end the suffering of a dying patient.

Meanwhile in Oregon in the United States, the state's voters
approved Measure 16 on 8 November 1994, which allows people
who expect to live less than six months to request a life-ending
dose of barbiturates. The prescription has to be approved by two
doctors and the patient has to place the drugs in his mouth
himself. A US judge has temporarily blocked the measure from
coming into effect, as he wants to hear arguments about whether
the law is constitutional. Elsewhere in the United States, the
Michigan Senate has approved by a vote of 26-9 a permanent
ban on Dr Jack Kevorkian's practice of counselling terminally ill
people about suicide. It now moves to the Michigan House of
Representatives for consideration. The doctor has helped 21
people to commit suicide since 1990. The only country where
doctor-assisted suicide is now available is Holland.

In Canada, the Canadian Medical Association Journal published calculations that Alzheimer's and other dementias cost
Canadians almost $4 billion a year. The figure is expected to rise
to at least $12 billion by 2031. Currently, such diseases account
for nearly six cents in every health-care dollar spent in Canada.
Over a quarter of a million who are past retirement age meet the

diagnostic criteria for dementia out of a total population of 25 million.

In light of the greying of the population of developed countries and because of the hideous escalation in the cost of medical care, the debate about euthanasia is hotting up. It is estimated that Americans on average spend two-thirds of everything they spend on health care in their entire lives in the last one or two years of their life.

The reality is that individuals are facing a cruel dilemma. Even as doctors find ways of extending people's lives by converting life-threatening diseases into chronic ailments treatable over a prolonged period, the cost of exploiting these new discoveries is making the manner in which people die very significant financially. In the UK, for example, a family can be ruined if one of their members has Alzheimer's. Heart attacks, on the other hand, are not only quick, but cheap: the inheritance is passed on. It seems perfectly reasonable, therefore, to offer people the modern equivalent of walking out into the snow, as we were taught old Eskimos did when they felt they had become too much of a burden on their community.

Yet the moral case against euthanasia remains strong. For where do you draw the line? Perhaps the patient requesting a lethal dose of drugs is only temporarily depressed. And anyway, is it not a fundamental law of ethics (and part of the Hippocratic Oath too) that human life should be preserved at all costs and for as long as possible? And does one not encourage people to make morally wrong decisions by opening the door a little?

Two cases illustrate the last point. On 5 December 1994, Cathie Wilkieson, a Canadian resident of Ontario, sat in her car with her son Ryan aged sixteen, who had cerebral palsy, and let carbon monoxide kill them both. She had just lost an appeal to the provincial government for more home-care assistance for Ryan. Three weeks earlier, a Saskatchewan farmer named Robert Latimer was convicted of second-degree murder for killing his twelve-year-old daughter Tracey in a vehicle with carbon monoxide. She had cerebral palsy too. If euthanasia has any chance of increasing the frequency of this type of action – parents taking the lives of their children, however sick – it should remain banned forever.

OJ

Even though many people think that the verdict in OJ's criminal trial demonstrated the weakness of the American legal system, I disagree. He subsequently lost the civil case where only balance of probability was required to prove him liable.

8.10.1995 The Trial of the Century is over. Orenthal James Simpson walks away a free man. Billions of words have been written and spoken about the "not guilty" verdict. What can one add?

Well, let's strip away the publicity surrounding the trial and consider it like any ordinary one. The two most important aspects of a criminal trial are causality and certainty. The whole reason for having a prosecution and a defence is that a jury can hear two opposing versions of the causal chain leading up to the crime – the one placing the defendant in the dock firmly in the causal chain as a participant and the other excluding him altogether. The jury is asked to hold the contrasting hypotheses in mind right up to the moment that they make the decision.

When they do make a decision, a criminal trial demands that the jury do more than balance the odds of one scenario against the odds of the other. For a jury to render a "guilty" verdict, they must be reasonably sure that the defendant committed the crime. If they give any credence at all to the "not guilty" scenario, then they must give the benefit of the doubt to the defendant and find him not guilty.

This is very different to the way we normally think in the world outside the courtroom. When we consider whether somebody is to blame for something or not, we go on the balance of probability. If we are 51 per cent certain that the person did perpetrate the offence, it's good enough. The person is admonished. Indeed, in our ordinary world of prejudice and emotion, one finds wishful thinking creeping in at times. In this event, it only has to be a possibility of guilt (i.e. less than a 50 per cent chance) for a judgement to be made against an individual. That is what drives lynch mobs to dispense instant justice on victims who are often innocent. That is what political show trials are all about.

Modern legal systems quite rightly have nothing to do with these methods of justice. They impose the much stricter criteria to which I referred earlier when imposing criminal liability. Hence, people are often confused by "not guilty" verdicts in trials because they are applying everyday logic, emotion and prejudice in the wrong context. In Simpson's case, the evidence was circumstantial. There was no actual eyewitness. Circumstantial evidence must be overwhelming to get a "guilty" verdict. All the defence had to do was sow the smallest seed of doubt about the integrity of the evidence being led by the prosecution for a "not guilty" verdict to be assured.

This they did successfully. Despite all the physical evidence which appeared to incriminate Simpson, including the famous bloody glove, despite all the DNA tests on the blood found at the crime scene, in Simpson's car and at his home, which experts claimed to have his as well as the victims' genetic markers, the defence simply played an alternative scenario. The glove was planted, Simpson was framed, the case was mishandled. With the revelations of the racist character of one of the policemen central to the case – Mark Furhrman – the alternative scenario gained some plausibility. It didn't need more than that.

So forget about all the other issues like the racial composition of the jury, the legal resources Simpson could muster for the trial, etc., etc. The verdict reflects the way the legal system works in America. Nobody has come up with anything better. A person is innocent till proved guilty beyond reasonable doubt. If you were in the dock, you would want it that way too.

Liberal Dilemma

The criminals are as barbaric as they ever were. How do we make them fear retribution without resorting to medieval-type punishments?

13.11.1994 As the world turns, an elderly woman does her normal morning shopping in a Sussex village in England. She returns to find her house being stripped bare by a gang from London using a pantechnicon to remove her belongings. She is badly beaten up. Meanwhile, some Scandinavian kids club one of their own to death. A sniper's bullet claims a pedestrian in a town somewhere in Bosnia. The Russian mafia dispose of an unaccommodating entrepreneur in Moscow. A gunman runs amok in China. An Australian politician investigating the underworld is shot. Another drive-by shooting claims the life of an eleven-year-old boy in America. And a church leader is murdered in front of his grandchildren in South Africa.

As Gary Edwards, co-host of Radio 702's morning show, said on the air last Monday: "Violence is awfully universal." He is right. Despite a recent chart in *The Economist* showing that the level of crime per capita is no worse in London now than it was at the beginning of the century, most law-abiding Londoners as well as most of us here in South Africa feel overwhelmed by the sheer viciousness as well as the frequency of criminal acts.

It may be – to use the title of Hollywood's latest action movie – that mankind has always had its share of "natural born killers", those who take other people's lives to assert their own existence. It may be that the media is just bringing this fact to our attention in a more repetitive way than was conceivable a few decades ago. The cameras get to the scene of the crime quicker, the photographs of the carnage are sharper.

Whatever the true position, each outrageous act of theft, rape, carjacking, murder, etc. poses a tougher dilemma for people of a liberal persuasion. For we believe in the utilitarian theory of punishment. It should be an act of rehabilitation, not of retribution. No eye for an eye. Therefore the death penalty and corporal punishment are considered obscene and cruel. We also believe in the due process of law where a person is innocent until proven guilty beyond reasonable doubt. Thirdly, we believe that in the longer run crime can only be diminished by getting rid of unemployment, by improving housing, hospitals and schools, and by reaffirming the family as the basic unit of society where children learn their moral values.

The nub of the dilemma is this. While liberals are happy to see the system of justice the world over more and more reflecting their values, they are uncomfortably aware that ordinary folk are moving in exactly the opposite direction. To them, the system has gone cockeyed. Moreover, the reason behind such a counter movement is one that liberals cannot argue with: anger and resentment caused by the curtailment of personal liberty. When people are afraid to go out of doors, children can never be left alone, gangs of thugs reign supreme in the streets, the only protection is a gun, a fierce dog, burglar bars, electronic surveillance devices and high walls, we all realise something has gone dreadfully wrong. When a renowned judge in England argues that homeowners should be taken to court if their homes are burgled on the grounds that insufficient security tempted the criminal to commit the crime, we would go further and say, like the Yorkshireman, that the world is daft.

Politicians, sensing the frustration of the population, are using law and order as the number one ticket for election. In most countries, jails are over-crowded even as more new jails are being built than new schools. So what is the solution? I can only give the obvious one: in the short run, more police and greater support of the police by the community in their role of preventing crime and bringing criminals to justice; in the long run, social upliftment. The worst thing to do, however, is to shrug our shoulders and says it's the state's problem. All of us have to contribute towards a law-abiding culture. As John Donne, the seventeenth century metaphysical poet, wrote: "Any man's death diminishes me, because I am involved in Mankind; and therefore never send to know for whom the bell tolls; it tolls for thee."

Hung Jury

Hence, when we still had a death penalty in South Africa, I was am-
bivalent about it.

26.2.1995 Whenever emotion runs high in any war of words, each side is bound to portray the other side in less than truthful terms. Such is the case with the current public debate over capital punishment. The "abolitionists" label the "retentionists" as cruel, bloodthirsty hang-'em-high reactionaries. The retentionists typecast their opponents as lily-livered liberals always siding with the downtrodden criminal against the aggrieved victim.

Where do the two sides genuinely part company on this vexing issue? I do not think the difference lies any more in either side's attitude towards serious crime like murder and rape. Both will agree that it has got out of hand in South Africa and something has to be done about it. The disagreement revolves around the "something to be done".

The retentionist will argue that since fear is the best means of restraining unacceptable human behaviour and nobody fears anything worse than death, for extreme crimes death is the most effective punishment. Moreover, it satisfies society's need for retribution: an eye for an eye. Rehabilitation – the granting of a second chance – is therefore inappropriate. To the counter-argument that where the death penalty is applied in the United States it has done nothing to reduce crime, the retentionist will respond that the complexity and drawn-out nature of the appeal process nullify the deterrence value of capital punishment. In other countries, such as some in the Middle and Far East where execution is swift and seen to be swift, the level of murder and rape is almost negligible (abolitionists would ascribe this to the strict moral code of Islam and Confucius).

As far as the morality of capital punishment is concerned, retentionists will contend that there already exist circumstances in which the killing of another human being is condoned. Examples are self-defence and the waging of a just war, the second motive being responsible for the deaths of hundreds

108

of thousands of innocent civilians. Dresden, Hiroshima and Nagasaki come to mind. Extending the list of acceptable conditions from the aforementioned to the killing of murderers is not breaking new philosophical ground at all. In fact, the retentionist will claim that it is a contradiction to approve the collective killing of innocent persons under one set of conditions, while disapproving the killing of a guilty person under another set.

A diametrically opposed position is taken by abolitionists on the issue of morality. There is the pure pacifist's line that the killing of fellow human beings is evil under all circumstances. Hence, any deliberate killing of soldier and civilian alike in wartime or peacetime is reprehensible. This position is logically unassailable if you accept the premise.

The more common and qualified line taken by abolitionists is that there is a critical difference between peace and a just war. The killing of people in the latter may be necessary, but no grounds – other than self-defence – can be put forward for killing people in peacetime. The validity of this view rests on the perception that the same act can be moral or immoral depending on the circumstances surrounding it.

Abolitionists will buttress their position by adding that execution is irreversible and mistakes as to the identity of the murderer can be and have been made. Moreover, a certain arbitrariness always surrounds the sentencing of a condemned criminal to death because it is a subjective opinion as to whether extenuating circumstances existed at the time or not. Finally, as an alternative deterrent to the death penalty, a portion of abolitionists would opt for "effective life imprisonment" in the case of cold-blooded murder. This means no chance of remission for good behaviour. The rest of your life is spent in jail. You die in jail. Again, there is no question of rehabilitation – only containment. Some abolitionists would say this is going too far. All punishment should offer some prospect of rehabilitation. Retentionists, on the other hand, would object that effective life imprisonment would cost the state too much and you can never eliminate the chance of escape altogether.

Like all debates of this nature, the side you're on very much depends on your fundamental beliefs. These vary from individual to individual. This poses the subsidiary question as to whether a small body of intelligent experts should make the final decision on the death penalty or the matter should be subjected to a referendum. If the latter, I shall exercise my right to a secret ballot.

My Verdict
But so many recent reversals of death sentences in America have convinced me that the re-introduction of capital punishment in South Africa would be wrong – however tempting.

2.11.1997 Occasionally, a single statistic acts like a speeding bullet. It cuts down an opposing argument by leaving a neat hole in it. I discovered one such statistic in a recent edition of *The Economist*. It goes like this: "In all, 69 Americans condemned to death have been freed after new evidence disproved their guilt since 1973, 21 since 1993." The article continues: "Is the system getting better at recognising its mistakes? Alas, it may still be condemning too many people too quickly to execution in the first place."

Good grief! Sixty-nine people had their death sentences reversed in a country that prides itself on the quality of its legal system. You may argue that the appeal process worked; but what happened in the original trials? Was the jury hasty? Did the witnesses lie? Was the evidence tampered with? Or did clever prosecutors run rings around a defence team which was not as good as OJ's because the defendant couldn't afford it?

Let us consider a case from Illinois described in the same article. Dennis Williams and his co-defendant Verneal Jimerson were both awaiting execution in 1996, having spent seventeen years on death row for a double murder. By chance, a Northwestern University professor asked four of his students to look into their case as part of their course in investigative journalism. They discovered that the key witness had been fed details of the crime by the police. They uncovered a police file suggesting that four other men may have committed the crime though none had been interviewed. One was dead, but due to the students' investigation the other three eventually confessed to the crime. At the same time, Williams and Jimerson were exonerated by DNA tests which were previously not allowed. Depending on how you look at it, they were lucky to get off or unlucky to have spent so long in purgatory because the law was manipulated against them.

I remember once watching the movie *10 Rillington Place* with Richard Attenborough playing the infamous mass murderer, John Christie. It was based on the true story of an innocent man, Timothy Evans, convicted in England in 1959 of brutally murdering his family. When it was subsequently proven that Christie had done the foul deed, the public outrage over the execution of an innocent man caused the death penalty to be repealed in Great Britain.

I've always assumed that it was extremely rare for the wrong man to have gone to the gallows or the electric chair for "murder one". But the article plainly shows that "beyond reasonable doubt" is in no way equivalent to absolute certainty. In any judgement, no matter how cast iron the evidence, the chances of human error always exist. Judges and juries are mortal like the rest of us – particularly in the case of murders where the victims are not around to offer direct testimony. If only one innocent man is punished with death at the hands of the state, that is extremely bad news. He can't be brought back. To guard against this, a lengthy appeal process is obligatory, but it can never be foolproof and it detracts from the value of execution as a deterrent.

At a time when calls for a referendum on reinstituting the death penalty in South Africa are being renewed, ask yourself this question. Can you honestly say you're in favour of it if we run the risk of scrambling a few innocent eggs in the course of making a law-and-order omelette?

Oklahoma City and Atlanta

The power of governments to impose their will is slipping.

4.8.1996 In my column at the beginning of November 1995, I made the following observation: "The most important internal trend is the destabilising effect of subnational organisations carving out empires of their own within each state. Such organisations include clans, terrorist groups, religious cults, private militias, urban gangs and rural bandits." I was echoing the words of Martin Van Crefeld, a military historian at the Hebrew University of Jerusalem.

To the car bomb in Oklahoma City last year we must now add a pipe bomb which left two dead and 112 injured at the Olympic Games in Atlanta. Once again the helplessness of a modern society in the face of fanatics who want to kill or maim innocent people has been revealed. No longer "pulp fiction", we have a "pulp future" threatening us.

The problem is twofold. Firstly, we have seen an unprecedented growth in global population in this century. People forget that, for thousands of years, the world's population could be measured in hundreds of millions. Now we're approaching six billion, which means that over one-sixth of all the people who have lived since the birth of Christ are alive today.

It is pretty safe to assume that the proportion of really evil people among mankind has remained constant throughout history. It certainly hasn't diminished. That means that they're far more numerous now. The ones that go beyond thinking evilly to committing an evil deed are harder to find. The needle is now located in a huge haystack and, with modern forms of travel, it can change position more quickly too. The intelligence network required to identify, let alone capture, individuals responsible for terrorist acts therefore needs to be awesome.

Secondly, we are experiencing an unprecedented vacuum of authority in the world. This may sound surprising in an age where the rich nations have nuclear weapons. But the kind of global disorder that exists requires a totally different form of control. We no longer have hierarchical structures like empires where peace was once imposed on a large area of the globe by an imperial authority situated in Athens, Rome, Constantinople, London or latterly Moscow. The only real superpower left, America, is ever more unwilling to spill the blood of her youth on foreign soil. Neither the wars in Vietnam and the Gulf nor the expedition into Somalia (where the troops arrived after CNN) provide happy reminiscences to the American public. The media have made the horrors of war far more visible to American mothers. The upshot is that America's direct interests have to be severely threatened for the despatch of troops overseas to be justified in the public eye.

Internally, governments have less control over their populations. Modern-day values which emphasise the freedom and rights of the individual make authoritarian structures less and less acceptable. Of relevance here is the contradiction between "state intelligence", which implies covert activities but which is vital to track down the terrorists, and the growing popularity of the principle of transparency in everything that the state does.

So we have two record-breaking aspects in the world: the highest number of evil people around with the least level of authority to control them. Add to this the fact that in four years' time more than half the world's population will be clustered in cities and towns and therefore more susceptible to terrorist acts. It's a lethal mixture and the stuff of nightmare scenarios.

Mafiosi

At the same time, the power of the Mafiosi is increasing.

28.5.1995 When Moscow television journalist Vladislav Listyev stopped an assassin's bullet earlier this year, he was investigating the increasing criminalisation of Russian society. In Russia alone it is estimated that 5 000 criminal groups exist, of which 200 are large criminal syndicates extending beyond Russia's borders and linked to the Italian Cosa Nostra, Asian Triads and Columbian drug syndicates.

Although the repressive power structures of the previous

Soviet Union have been dismantled, many of the apparatchiks who were members of those structures have merely shifted their allegiance to or joined the Russian Mafia. The Mafia now dominates Russian society the way the Communist Party and KGB used to do from 1917 to 1990. The totalitarianism is still there, but the dictators have changed into godfathers. One of the latter has his own army of a thousand private security guards. When he wants his will enforced, he uses tanks not guns. Politicians, businessmen and journalists are all fair game for the dons of the Russian Mafia. The difference between the Italian and the Russian Mafia is that the former disregards the law whereas the latter believes it is the law.

In Sicily, the home of the original Mafia, a war has erupted between current Mafiosi and ex-members who have broken "omerta" – the vow of silence – to turn in their colleagues to the police. The carnage of hits and counter hits has converted the country back into a network of frightened villages. The blistering sun contrasts with the subdued black robes of the mourners in the almost daily funeral processions.

In the United States, home to Al Capone and other legendary mobsters who used to sport wide-brimmed fedoras, chalk-striped suits, silk shirts and spats, the locals no longer have the lion's share of the streets. James Cagney, if he were still alive, would not be the automatic choice for the leading role of villain in a modern gangster movie. Crime has become truly internationalised. Every conceivable nationality is represented, fighting vicious turf wars with far more sophisticated weapons than the tommy guns used by mobsters in the Roaring Twenties. The product mix has altered too: drugs followed by gambling, with prostitution running a poor third. Alcohol, the staple commodity of the Protection era, has long since been legalised; the speakeasy is now a singles bar.

Worldwide, the criminal underground is extending its tentacles. Drugs are pivotal to that process. Some of the most powerful players are the Columbian cartels who purchase farmers' coca leaves from various parts of South America. They operate laboratories, hidden deep in tropical forests, that refine

114

the coca into pure cocaine. They wholesale the product to the innumerable distribution rings in American cities who water it down and multiply the price.

The Columbian drug czars are so powerful that they basically rule Medellin, Bogota and the rural areas of Columbia, despite everything that the US and Columbian governments are doing to destroy them. The organisation is a many-headed hydra – one boss is cut down and plenty of others crop up to replace him. The czars are seen by many Columbians as modern Robin Hoods, exploiting rather than robbing rich Americans. They help the poor by allocating a percentage of the drugs money to build schools and hospitals and uplift whole communities. Elsewhere in South America, they masquerade as resistance movements fighting a just war against repressive regimes.

The barbarians are no longer at the gates. They're inside. They go under different names, but they're all Mafiosi. They hold the common citizenry in sway by fear (Sicily) or by a combination of fear and charity (Columbia). Three of the biggest countries in the world – China, Russia and America – are falling victim to their evil influence. With South Africa rejoining the world economy, there are already signs that some of the first international investors are the drug syndicates. This can only strengthen the local network of gangs that unfortunately dominate the lives of so many of our poorer citizens. Are we going to allow this to happen?

Pax Americana
So, from every angle, the Americans are finding it less and less easy to keep peace in the world.

12.4.1998 The Romans had a straightforward foreign policy for enforcing Pax Romana. They offered the people they conquered two options: either co-operate and be a useful part of the Roman Empire or be annihilated by the legions. Unsurprisingly, most chose the first option and Europe had the longest peace in its history.

Now we have Pax Americana but under very different diplomatic rules. For a start, empires are out and individual nationhood is in. Whereas the Romans could walk into any country they liked without consulting anybody, the Americans are under pressure to obtain the approval of the United Nations before they send the troops in. And even if they get it, it's on the basis of a temporary sojourn – not a permanent fixture.

Secondly, we live today in a world of human rights and international media networks. Reporters have usually set up camp in the target country even before the invasion has begun. Any bloodshed – particularly unnecessary bloodshed – will be broadcast within hours to every corner of the globe. Caesar wrote about the Roman campaigns in Gaul very much from the point of view of the victor. Nobody quarrelled with his version of history. There weren't photographs of the opposition's butchered bodies and harrowing interviews with the survivors to provide an alternative perspective. There were no charges of racism or of the First World dominating the Third World. Caesar returned to Rome in triumph, not to face a Senate hearing on his conduct during the war.

These modern restraints effectively stop America from doing anything rash and inhuman in the course of carrying out its peacemaking duties. Most of us would regard this as a good thing. Nevertheless, one must bear in mind that the world is still an unstable place. There are plenty of nasty dictators around who are quite capable of stirring up trouble in their neighbourhood. Moreover, the one dramatic change in world affairs since Roman times is the advent of weapons of mass destruction. We've moved from the sword which could slay one person at a time to nuclear, biological and chemical warheads which can kill thousands of people in one blow.

That's why it would be foolish to write off the second encounter between the US and Saddam Hussein as a nice way for Bill Clinton to gain extra support during his second presidential term. Much more is at stake. My guess is that Saddam has already developed an intermediate-range missile capability which can plant a nasty warhead not just on Tel Aviv but also on London or

Paris. Of course, given the amount of time he's been given to clear out the arms from his palaces, no shred of evidence to support this thesis will be found. It's a case of hide and seek, after the seeker has counted to a hundred and announced where he is going to look. But even if I'm wrong, there are bound to be other Saddams in the new millennium who want to test the limits of superpower endurance and at the same time possess the potential to wipe out huge numbers of people in faraway lands.

What can America or its allies do? Wait for a shower of incoming missiles before launching a retaliatory strike – in which case some hostile warheads may elude the antimissile net and cause great harm to their own citizens? Or launch a pre-emptive strike to neutralise the risk before it materialises – in which case they face the possibility of alienating a large segment of the world's population? Not an easy choice. Life for the Roman emperors was simple by comparison.

Huntington versus Fukuyama
But age-old religious divisions and national antagonisms don't change.

4.1.1998 Two books, which are poles apart, have recently been written on the future evolution of cultures. On the one hand, *The End of History* by Francis Fukuyama proclaims that culturally the world is converging on Western values and the free-market ethic; the ideological battle between West and East and certainly between capitalism and communism is over; and from now on therefore, history is going to be pretty boring because the only issue is which country is grabbing a greater share of this or that world market. Everybody will be homogenised by commerce and trade.

Not so, says Samuel Huntington. In his book, *The Clash of Civilizations*, he takes a diametrically opposed view. We're about to witness the all-time heavyweight contest in world history between Western values, Islam and Confucianism. Each is girding its loins to dominate the new millennium.

Staking out the extremes, as these two authors have done, is no bad thing because it promotes debate in the centre. But, in deliberately making their arguments one-dimensional for maximum effect, they skate over the complexity of life. For example, Fukuyama's hypothesis more or less rules out another major conflict, while Huntington's implies that it will be precipitated by cultural or religious differences. Actually, the age-old motives of power and greed could be the cause of the next great war.

Nevertheless, where Fukuyama is correct is that if you visit Moscow, Beijing, Hanoi, Bombay and even Havana, the young are decked out in Levis and short slinky dresses; they dance the night away in discos to the sounds of the Spice Girls; and they have the same material ambitions and the same problems with drugs. Western consumerism is everywhere. It is therefore very easy to be taken in by articles on the subject in Western newspapers and journals that this trend means everything to the future of this planet. The great, global, homogenised teenager is going to be our saviour because he or she has conveniently absorbed Western values and artefacts.

However, below the sheen, Huntington's anxieties are warranted. None of the different religions or philosophies which are current among large sections of mankind has changed one iota as a result of greater contact between the peoples of this Earth. Not one word of the Bible, the Koran or the Torah has been amended since it was first written. Not a single saying of Buddha or Confucius has been modified. Nor is this ever likely to change, because the essence of The Truth is that it remains unaltered.

So where do we go from here? No doubt the spreading of capitalism throughout the world (a correct assumption in Fukuyama's book) is going to lead to a redistribution of economic power away from Western nations to nations representing the other cultures of the world. Hence, in the next century, it is going to be harder for Westerners to impress their beliefs on the others unless they are already universally accepted. Proselytising agencies like Amnesty International and Greenpeace will face a tougher uphill task in getting their messages across about banning capital punishment and environmentally dangerous practices when Western clout starts to disappear and viewpoints become more relative. Asian nations are already complaining about having Western standards foisted on them. Indeed, they see these standards as a camouflaged attempt by the bullying West to preserve the gap between advanced and developing economies – a subtle way of undermining their competitiveness.

Whether all this potential for cultural conflict boils over into a war would be pure surmise. But history is going to be anything but boring. That is where Huntington is right and Fukuyama is wrong.

Chechnya
The war in Chechnya clearly demonstrated the lethal quality of angry minorities.

15.1.1995 Alvin Toffler made the prophetic observation many years ago that the greatest potential for conflict in society lay with minorities. The current bid by one million Chechens to liberate themselves from 150 million Russians is a case in point. The conflict around and in Grozny, the capital of Chechnya, has already claimed sufficient lives of soldiers and civilians to be classified as a war – ceasefire or no ceasefire.

Several decades ago, such an insurrection would have been put down by the former Soviet Union very quickly and with maximum force. Any Chechens with ambitions about independence would have played this scenario through their minds beforehand and been deterred – indeed were deterred – from taking action. But times have changed. Russia is a democracy where political opponents of Boris Yeltsin have had a field day questioning his judgement every step of the way in this war. Nightly, Russian television has been relaying gory and distressing pictures from the Chechen front to Muscovite mothers who feel it is pointless to have young men risk their lives for this cause. Even the Russian army is ambivalent about some of the manoeuvres they are being ordered to make. When Chechen civilians stand in front of their tanks, they stop.

Then there are the international news networks providing eyewitness accounts of the growing civilian casualties as a result of indiscriminate bombing. Bloody footsteps in the snow, make-shift operating theatres in rundown hospitals, a father grieving over his infant son's death – these are images which Stalin would never have allowed to be beamed into households around the world.

It all adds up to one conclusion. The days are gone when a country can be held together by sheer force and terror. Tyrants can no longer sweep their dirty little deeds under the carpet and appear to be cuddly and lovable to those fortunate enough to live outside their thrall. There's no such thing as a compulsory unitary state or a compulsory federal state either. If a minority wants out, it can thumb its nose at the majority under the relative security of international publicity and declare itself out. If the majority tries to maintain its hegemony over the unwilling minority, it will either be internationally isolated if it uses too much force or face an interminable guerilla war if it uses too little. Turkey faces this dilemma with the Kurds.

The Economist put it thus: "As a go-it-alone country of about one million people, Chechnya, even with oil, may find any independence it wins to be illusory. That, however, is a matter for the Chechens. If they wish to divorce in haste, they can repent at leisure. For Mr Yeltsin the important lesson is to understand that democracies cannot be glued together by force."

So how can a country remain undivided and whole these days? The answer is that the rulers must convince the minorities that the country is a club of which membership is desirable. This will happen when the economic benefits associated with belonging to such a club are perceived to outweigh any loss of political sovereignty that goes with such membership. It sounds simple, but it's quite a tall order, bearing in mind how seductive the clarion call of nationalism can be. For example, French-speaking Quebec is once again considering whether it wants to be part of Canada or not – even though Canada is one of the most advanced and stable democracies in the world today. Furthermore, Norwegians voted to remain outside the European Union.

As the voices of discontent in Natal once again rumble ominously like a distant thunderstorm in the Drakensberg, all parties in South Africa would do well to refrain from acting in haste. We cannot afford to repent at our leisure, because any major internal row now will make overseas investors leave their wallets in their back pockets for good. It is surely not in the interests of any province to separate itself from South Africa. But then it is up to the South African government to prove that this is so.

France's Nuclear Trigger

And now we have the new round of underground testing of nuclear weapons, starting with France.

25.6.1995 A decade is defined for each person by a handful of personalities, one or two events, some personal experiences, etc. The sixties for me were Harold Wilson smoking his pipe, Christine Keeler's involvement with John Profumo, the Beatles (obviously), the death of JFK, my first office job, getting married. But one activity which always concerned me from my earliest days of becoming conscious about the world beyond England was the testing of nuclear weapons.

Seeing those tests on black-and-white TV – the blinding light followed by the mushroom cloud emanating from some obscure atoll in the Pacific – made me feel insecure. I had learnt Einstein's Law in Physics "A" level class at school: energy equals mass times the square of the velocity of light ($E = mc^2$). However, it was almost incomprehensible that a minute reduction in mass could be related to a huge flash of energy by something as totally exotic as the speed of light. Yet simple mathematical equations based on the premise that the speed of light is constant in all directions and in all frameworks of reference were indisputably true. Einstein's special theory of relativity was a brilliant piece of work because you didn't need a PhD in mathematics to follow his logic. But it did lead to some weird conclusions – objects speeding past you at close to the speed of light were measured to be heavier and shorter, clocks ticked more slowly and mass could be converted into energy and vice versa. The last conclusion was verified long before the tests I watched on TV. The US Manhattan Project which led to the two atom bombs dropped on Nagasaki and Hiroshima was undertaken in the early 1940s. The bombs were an incredibly fearful and devastating result of such a neat little equation.

What stirs these memories is France's decision to resume nuclear testing, ending a moratorium placed on such activity by President Mitterrand in 1992. Unlike his predecessor, President Chirac is prepared to risk the wrath of Far Eastern countries like Japan, Australia and New Zealand in order to guarantee the effectiveness of the French nuclear arsenal. One New Zealand Government backbencher, Mr Brian Neeson, said: "I bare my backside to France and those who have made this decision." He kept his insult verbal. More seriously, the French Consulate in Perth, Western Australia, has been burnt down, apparently set alight in an act of arson.

It must be said that France is undertaking a limited number of tests (eight) between September this year and May next year and they will all be underground explosions. The 56 residents of Pitcairn Island – mainly descendants of the 1789 mutineers of the *Bounty* and 800 kilometres from France's chosen site of Mururoa Atoll – are relatively unfazed. Tom Christian, a direct descendant of midshipman Fletcher Christian who led the seizure of *HMS Bounty* and set Captain William Blight adrift, said by satellite phone from Pitcairn: "There has been no real talk about them (the tests) here. It isn't really worrying people."

Nevertheless, one does feel queasy about any nation testing its nuclear weapons on exactly the opposite side of the globe from its own self, however safe the procedures are. Imagine what French citizens would say if the Americans had agreed with the Channel Islands to do some further underground testing there. The reaction would be passionate. Another problem is that if one nation starts updating its nuclear arsenal, then according to the MAD rationale (mutually assured destruction) every other nation possessing nuclear weapons has to do the same to keep the balance. Are these tests going to precipitate a new round of costly modernisations to the existing global pile of nuclear weapons which are already capable of blowing mankind sky-high? On the other hand, dear old Einstein with his straggly white hair and avuncular look might argue that his equation is the principal reason we haven't had another world war. Nations will always seek improvements to their position which will be counterbalanced by the others. This is how peace is achieved. But I hark back to my uneasy feelings as a schoolboy. If the wrong finger is ever resting on the nuclear trigger, what then? Knowledge is indestructible, people aren't.

Another Big Bang?
Pakistan and India quickly followed suit.

16.8.1998 In *The New Century*, a book published at the beginning of this decade, I floated the following scenario: "The nuclear risk also applies to any conflict between Pakistan and India over disputed territory on their borders." More recently, in an article in this newspaper, I alluded to the relative powerlessness of modern Americans compared to ancient Romans and how difficult it was to be a global cop these days.

Well, the nuclear risk has notched up a few extra degrees of probability this year. In making this so, India and Pakistan have given a fresh definition to the phrase "high five". Instead of a mutual palm-slapping gesture of applause, they matched each other's batch of underground nuclear tests in the spirit of "anything you can do, I can do too".

Predictably, the Americans and other nuclear-haves are outraged at this new act of proliferation and have imposed sanctions on both countries. Predictable too is the response that the nuclear powers are indulging in the worst type of hypocrisy. If they have nuclear weapons, why can't everybody else have them too? What makes them so special that they alone should be entrusted with the ultimate explosive?

The problem is that, even if the entire world officially destroyed every nuclear weapon in existence, the knowledge of how to make another one would still be there. The risk remains that someone somewhere could start another clandestine stockpiling programme. After all, the information on how to manufacture a nuclear device is available on the Internet.

So where to from here? The stakes are high, as environmentalists will tell you. A substantial exchange of nuclear weapons could put the world into a temporary ice age because of the dust and the haze caused by the explosions blocking out the sun. This is apart from the radioactive fallout which could be spread by the prevailing winds.

The irony is that such a nasty scenario could be precipitated by Murphy's Law – anything that can go wrong will go wrong. Historians who've combed over the Cuban missile crisis, when America and the Soviet Union came within a hair's-breadth of starting the Third World War, have revealed one quality which permeated the whole incident – ignorance. Despite their intelligence networks, both sides were woefully unaware of the other's true positions, intentions and tactics. We could have blundered into a nuclear war.

The possibility of misidentification is still there. If a Boeing 747 strays unannounced into Indian air space, the authorities have a minute or two to decide whether it's an incoming Pakistani missile or indeed a peaceful civilian craft. Will there be a hot line between the rulers and, even if there is, will they trust one another?

The only body that can lay down some new rules for the nuclear game is the United Nations. An amended nonproliferation treaty will have to be negotiated. I doubt, though, that the West, Russia or China is prepared to dismantle their entire nuclear armoury to get an agreement that's binding on all parties. There'll always be an anxiety that such a move will render peaceful, law-abiding nations defenceless against some rogue dictator who doesn't play according to the rules.

So never underestimate human folly. The world started with a Big Bang; perhaps it will end with one too.

Hiroshima

Perhaps we should all remember exactly what happened at Hiroshima and Nagasaki.

6.8.1995 "It blasted; it pounced; it bored its way right through you. It was a vision which was seen with more than the eye. It was seen to last forever. You would wish it to stop; altogether it lasted about two seconds. Finally it was over, diminishing, and we looked toward the place where the bomb had been; there was an enormous ball of fire which grew and grew and it rolled as it grew; it went up into the air, in yellow flashes and into scarlet and green. It looked menacing. It seemed to come toward one."

Thus did Isidor Rabi, a brilliant physicist, describe how he felt when witnessing the test of the first atomic bomb. It occurred at 05:29 and 45 seconds on the morning of 16 July 1945. It took place in New Mexico, USA, on a desert plain known as Jornado del Muerto – dead man's journey. The blast equalled 18 600 tons of TNT. "My dad thought the steam locomotive had blown up" was the comment made by another witness who as a lad had been waiting for a pre-dawn train in the nearby town of Ancho.

That was the rehearsal for what happened fifty years ago today on 6 August 1945: the dropping of "Little Boy" on Hiroshima at 08:15 in the morning. Lt. Colonel Paul Tibbets, the pilot of the Enola Gay, the B-29 that dropped the bomb, wrote: "A bright light filled the plane. We turned back to look at Hiroshima. The city was hidden by that awful cloud, boiling up, mushrooming." His co-pilot Robert Lewis wrote: "My God, what have we done?" Around 70 000 men, women and children died instantly and an additional 130 000 died within months of radiation poisoning and burns.

One young ensign, Osborn Elliott, on the heavy cruiser *Boston* of the US Third Fleet visited Hiroshima a few weeks later. In his letter home, he said: "The city is/was situated in a valley – on the one side the mountains, on the other the sea. As you stand in the middle of town, for miles on every side nothing rises above the level of your knees except for the shell of a building or the grotesque skeleton of a tree or perhaps a mound where the rubble has been pushed into a pile. We saw a fire station in relatively good condition. But inside, the two fire trucks were caricatures of twisted metal. Scattered through the ruins are cash registers, typewriters, bicycles, safes, all oxidised beyond recognition by the heat. Many bottles had been partially melted and twisted into fantastic forms. A couple of miles from Ground Zero, two trolleys lay on their sides, along with some cars that had been hurled off the street. Small concrete buildings were swollen out of shape – including a church whose walls bulged outwards and whose bell tower formed an S-curve. In a residential district, someone's clothes dangled from a blackened tree branch. By contrast, a near-by shrine appeared untouched by the blast.

"One big building near the centre of town once had a large dome. The building was a shell, and nothing was left of the dome except the curved metal frames.

"How anybody was left alive, I do not know. But here and there, women and children were sitting on the rubble that was once their homes. We didn't see many wounded – just a few on crutches or with bandages on their heads. Many people had sores on their faces. We stared at them, and they gazed blankly at us."

These eyewitness accounts give graphic testimony to the terrible aftermath of a nuclear explosion (which nowadays would be even worse with a hydrogen bomb). My wife and I visited Hiroshima in September 1990. It is like Canberra in Australia – everything is recent. A museum in the Peace Park had photographs of the city taken soon after the explosion. It also exhibited a schoolgirl's burnt tunic as well as stones blackened by the heat but with the pale outline of human bodies which were standing against them at the time of the blast. Japanese families walked around us chatting animatedly about the exhibits. No trace of animosity existed in their voices. Equally, there was no blame assigned in the museum for the bombing. The only message was that it should never happen again.

Perhaps this is the correct perspective. We weren't living then and experiencing the actual circumstances which led to the bomb. It's therefore foolish for us to be judgemental now.

Winners and Losers

The Japanese made a stunning comeback from the Second World War. But we live in a topsy-turvy world where they have become losers again. Don't count them out, though!

4.10.1998 How's this for a title of a book: *How a Loser Became a Winner and Turned into a Loser Again.* Or we could reverse the words: *How a Winner Became a Loser and Turned into a Winner Again.*

The first book would trace the history of Japan over the last fifty years and the second would be about America during the same period. It seems amazing how the fortunes of both countries have gone up and down like waves on the ocean – except that they have been completely out of step with one another. The peaks of America (1950s and now) have coincided with the troughs in Japan. The peak of Japanese hegemony (1970s and 1980s) corresponded with a long trough in American affairs.

This yo-yoing pattern, when examined more closely, provides a useful insight into human behaviour. After being defeated in the Second World War, Japan's economy was in ruins. As one leading Western expert said at the time: "The economic situation in Japan may be fundamentally so unsound that no policies, no matter how wise, can save her from slow economic starvation." But, as the proverb says, necessity is the mother of invention. The Japanese through incredible determination and a formidable work ethic pulled themselves up by their own bootstraps. Firstly, they played a catch-up game using Western technology to produce cheap transistor radios and cars. Then they pushed the frontiers of industry forward with such inventions as zero-defect production processes and just-in-time stores management. Meanwhile, they showered new products on the market like the VCR, the Walkman and the video camera.

The Americans, on the other hand, as victors of the war could do no wrong in the 1950s. They believed in themselves and in General Motors. The symbol of the decade was a flashy Chevrolet with enormous chrome bumpers and tail fins. Then came Vietnam, self-doubt, inflation and a stop-go economy. By the

1970s the American dream looked distinctly frayed at the edges with Japanese goods flooding into the American market. Observers were writing off the Americans as too short-term and opportunistic, while praising the Japanese for their long-term visionary strategies.

Now the tables are turned and it is precisely the flexibility of the Americans that has allowed them to re-assert their dominance of world markets. By contrast, the long-term and somewhat dogmatic perspective of the Japanese has been their undoing. It has led them into a multiplicity of projects which are highly geared with debt finance and which are underperforming in the short term. They are therefore suffering from a solvency crisis like most other Asian Tigers.

The hard times in the Far East look likely to continue into the next century. But it would be just as wrong to write off the Japanese making a comeback as it was to project a long-term American decline ten years ago. The fascinating thing about the human condition is that deprivation begets innovation and success breeds complacence. There's a self-balancing mechanism out there which ensures that we are constantly in a state of flux. Just when we think we're winners, we take our foot off the innovation and work ethic pedal. When we're losers, we put our foot down hard on it.

In that sense, maybe the toughness of the economic situation here is just the right prelude to the shift in mindset required to make South Africa into a winning nation by 2010. Of course, we could go down after that. But as one of my friends said: "It's much better to be a has-been than a never-was!"

Kobe Earthquake

The Japanese have always worried that an earthquake would halt their winning run. They were right in their timing, but other causes were responsible for Japan's current economic decline.

12.2.1995 A railway track pointing straight up to the sky like a big dipper sawn in half. Tangled wires hanging over a couple walking down a road that looks as if a hundred car bombs have detonated in it simultaneously. A four-storey office block tilting crazily into a pedestrian crossing as though it has crash-landed there. A truck flattened by the full weight of a falling motorway after the supporting pillars snapped.

Another motorway on its side zig-zagging through the city centre, its streetlights dangling like untidy strands of hair. A grey slablike building lying across an otherwise undamaged thorough-fare, the ground-floor contents strewn around and open to the sky. Derailed railway carriages looking like toys that a child has care-lessly thrown across his room. Distant fires making the buildings in the foreground blue and ghostly. A lone man walking across a pile of scrap and debris that once was a neat row of small houses. A primary school gymnasium transformed into a gigantic dor-mitory of sleeping survivors.

Normally dapper "salary men" in anoraks and jeans speaking anxiously on rows of hastily established outside phones. A family sitting bolt upright on wooden chairs on a sandy floor, the father gazing stoically into the middle distance, the daughter in white socks and school shoes, the mother and son wearing purple "trainers". An old man in pyjamas reaching out from a stretcher outside his demolished home towards other hands, one as old as his and wearing a wedding ring.

Lines of people you could bump into anywhere in suburbia holding crates of plastic bottles and other canisters, waiting patiently for that most elementary substance – water. Five pale-wooded coffins, with a sprig of green leaves topped by a white flower lying on their lids and small personal possessions scat-tered around.

And this wasn't the Big One. This earthquake – epicentre Awaji Island 30 kilometres from Kobe – measured 7,2 on the Richter scale. The estimated death toll in and around Kobe is 5 000 so far and damage is put as high as \$50 billion. The Big One, the repetition of which Japan is bracing for, occurred in 1923 and measured 8,2 (a difference of one means a great deal since the Richter scale is logarithmic). Called the Great Kanto Earthquake, it struck Tokyo and killed 140 000. An earthquake of similar magnitude in Tangshan, China, accounted for 242 000 dead in 1976.

What lessons can be drawn from Kobe? The first is that the latest technologies both in predicting seismicity and in alleviating the impact of seismicity still have a long way to go. As far as prediction is concerned, suppose a seismic network had been in place in Kobe which had indicated at the beginning of this year a rising probability of an earthquake. Would Kobe and its surrounding communities have been evacuated to avoid loss of life? Would all the industries have been shut down? If Kobe hadn't happened, how long would the authorities have waited before declaring a false alarm? These questions demonstrate just how efficient a seismic network would have to be for an incredibly costly decision to be taken by government to disrupt people's lives, and indeed for the people concerned to abide by that decision.

Regarding diminution of the earthquake's impact, it is clear that the shock absorbers built into the design and foundations of the buildings, motorways and other constructions in Kobe simply did not do the expected job. Part of this was due to the poor soil conditions of the area. Nevertheless, Japanese engineers must be disappointed that modern science did not achieve more. This is no reason for giving up on the ongoing challenge to improve safety, but it is certainly a case of going back to the drawing board.

The other important lesson of Kobe (and the recent floods in Europe) is the more general one that Planet Earth is at times a very dangerous and hostile place for mankind to be located. A megadisaster like this should teach us all that the wars we fight among ourselves as human beings are insane. To co-exist with Mother Nature in ever greater numbers is going to require our total attention, wisdom and energy. Distractions caused by infighting could ultimately be our downfall. Let Kobe be the lesson.

Japanese Banking Woes

One of the causes of Japan's decline is the mountain of bad debts at Japanese banks.

1.10.1995 If you're like me when you walk into a bank to withdraw some money, it doesn't cross your mind that it may not be there. In Japan, though, this disquieting feeling is spreading among customers. Mistrust in the banking system there began to grow after the liquidation of Cosmo, Japan's fifth largest credit union, at the end of July. This proved to be a minor precursor to the more recent collapse of Kizu, Japan's second largest credit union based in Osaka, and the liquidation of the Hyogo Bank in Kobe.

Thousands of depositors crowded into both institutions demanding that their cash be immediately returned to them. A 64-year-old widow recalled, as quoted in *Newsweek*: "I was so upset and in a hurry that I fell on the street. I told them that if I couldn't get my money out, I was going to hang myself." She was only consoled when the authorities gave her a promissory note covering her savings at Kizu. In one day alone, around 100 billion yen ($1 billion) was withdrawn from Kizu by depositors who panicked. It would appear that the public's money is safe now that the Finance Ministry has stepped in to restore order. But it was meanwhile revealed that 73 per cent of Cosmo's loans to outsiders were irrecoverable. The figures for Kizu and Hyogo were put at 57 per cent and 55 per cent respectively.

The malaise within the Japanese banking industry is widespread. The official estimated total of bad loans in the books of Japanese banks is about 50 trillion yen ($500 billion). This was the result of reckless lending, particularly to property and construction companies in the boom times of the late 1980s and the early 1990s. The bubble of property prices burst and construction activity fell away in the recession, leaving a trail of bad debt. No wonder then that Moody's, a credit rating agency in America, gave particularly poor ratings to fifty Japanese banks in a survey of 478 banks in 21 countries.

The situation is made worse by the fact that not only in Japan but around the world generally a diminishing proportion of money is being deposited in banks by companies and individuals. This is due to capital markets now offering so many other exciting alternatives to customers for investing their cash. These alternatives do not involve banks, as the investments can be made without such an intermediary.

Ten years ago one would have been astonished to hear mention of the possibility of a bank run in a country as successful and as well organised as Japan. Yet the unthinkable has happened, which demonstrates that nothing is ever risk-free. Whenever you put your money in the bank, you are placing your faith in the integrity and competence of the people who work there. Moreover, next time you hear somebody complain about being turned down by a bank manager for a loan because he can't furnish any guarantee of repayment, just remember – before you sympathise – it's your money that is being lent. If you're a depositor, you want the bank to be prudent. Don't you?

China
Next door to Japan, China is awakening.

27.8.1995 I'll never forget an American's intriguing insight into the US. It is called the Big Gorilla Theory. He asked me, "Where does the Big Gorilla sleep?" After consideration, I responded, "In the grass." He said, "No." "In the cave?" "No." "In the tree?" "No." So I gave up and he said, "The Big Gorilla sleeps where he wants to sleep."

The point he was trying to make was that America has behaved like a big gorilla for years. With the collapse of the Soviet Union, the only other gorilla which could compete at the time left town. But the 1990s has seen the awakening of another big gorilla – China. We've all heard of the sleeping giant and that the next century is reserved for China. However, the time frame has moved forward, particularly given China's sensational economic growth rate over the recent past.

Some of China's actions are making the rest of the world

nervous, such as the continuation of underground nuclear tests; the selling of nuclear technology to other nations, which contravenes the treaty on nonproliferation; the firing of missiles at a target close to Taiwan; the grabbing of islands in the South China Sea to demonstrate sovereignty over almost all of these waters including any oil that may lie underneath; and a noncompromising attitude towards the future of Hong Kong.

Relations between the new and the old gorilla are not good. The arrest in China of Harry Wu, a naturalised American dissident, on charges of spying, together with China's obvious hostility to Taiwan, has caused considerable upset in the US Congress. Talk in the media is now of how to contain China's expansionism. However, the effect of China's unpredictability on prospects for the Far East is probably the most important medium-term issue. The region has an image of a miraculous economic club with new members – Indonesia, Malaysia, Thailand, Vietnam – joining the original pathfinders of Japan, Hong Kong, Singapore and South Korea. Will this incredible run of wealth creation and cooperation end? Will the energies which have been used to expand peaceful trade be focused on more warlike ends as old antagonisms reassert themselves?

The removal of a belligerent Soviet Union from the Far East's western rim has altered many of the strategic alliances between the nations there. Ironically, the lessening threat from this source has promoted a degree of instability. The American presence is not so strong and the Philippines may rue the day they asked the American forces to leave the bases on their soil. Japan and America had a common interest in holding the Soviet Union at bay. However, a short while ago they avoided a full-scale trade war over cars and car parts by the skin of their teeth. Their relationship will continue to be strained. At no time in history have Japan and China both been strong powers at the same time. Rivalry between the two could send shock waves through the region. Into whose camp will the rest of the less powerful nations fall should they have to take sides?

To sum up, quite a large amount of uncertainty is building up in the Far East specifically and in the world generally with the emergence of the new Big Gorilla. This one has 20 per cent of the world's population. No superpower has ever had that kind of numerical domination. Unlike America, the new gorilla is not democratic, has problems of leadership and is still testing its strength against all the other animals in the jungle. However, it may not go so far as to spoil the Far Eastern miracle from which it obtains clear benefits. Everything could settle down or sparks could fly!

Russian Doll
The problem with Russia is that the Russian doll has gone and a liberal democracy takes time to grow. In between, things are pretty chaotic.

4.2.1996 It's the final countdown. South Africa will soon have a permanent constitution. But what model of power will it be based upon? There are too many loose ends to tell at this stage.

Basically there are two models of power around in the world – the Kremlin and the Liberal Democratic. To illustrate the former, picture an arrangement of Russian dolls. If you recall, they sit on top of each other. As each doll is lifted off, another one is revealed inside. The essence of this model is that the doll at the centre is the most powerful. Each outer doll depends for its status and authority on the doll immediately beneath it. Unsurprisingly, all dolls look alike.

In the former Kremlin, the President was the central doll. He was surrounded in concentric rings by the Politburo, the KGB, the armed forces, the Nomenklatura (the top party apparatchiks) and the Communist Party. This stack of dolls ruled the former Soviet Union with a rod of iron. Hierarchy was everything. Everyone knew their place in the chain and what to do. Power was considered a zero-sum game – if I win, you lose. Hence, there was no such thing as a loyal opposition. It had to be annihilated. The winner took all.

Despite its obvious flaws, in that absolute power corrupts absolutely and central planning doesn't work, the Kremlin model is still flourishing in some countries. It accords with man's primordial instinct to dominate. It also offers security of a sort to the masses. In its blatant form, it prevails in China and the Middle East. In disguise, one sees it in so-called democracies where the ruling parties win every election by seemingly impossible majorities. In Russia, though jettisoned by Yeltsin and the reformers, the model evokes nostalgia among a section of the general populace. They yearn for the good old days of law and order, strong leadership and superpower status. They are unhappy that, in exchange for the freedom to read dissident poetry, they can no longer walk in the streets for fear of criminals. It was therefore not a matter of chance that the Communist Party did so well in the recent parliamentary poll.

By contrast, inherent in the Liberal Democratic model is the idea that power should be diffused, or, pursuing the analogy, the dolls should be dispersed into smaller stacks independent of one another. Power comes from diversity, not sameness. Thus checks and balances are the essence of this model. These are brought about by different political parties competing for power, the executive and legislative branches of government being split, the independence of the central bank, the judiciary and the media being entrenched and local and provincial government receiving as much authority as can be devolved from the centre.

While the Liberal Democratic model causes more uncertainty in the short term than the Kremlin one because of contrarian ideas and rival factions jostling with one another in the marketplace, it is of much greater resilience in the longer term. This is primarily for one reason – it does not rely for its continuity on the personality of the person at the top, i.e. the central doll. America has survived some appalling presidents because the constitution was written with that danger in mind. On the other hand, the brittleness of the Soviet-Union and Yugoslavia was revealed when no leader of sufficient strength could be found to succeed predecessors of greater stature. One broke up peacefully, the other bloodily. Is there not a lesson in that for us?

Five Nobel Laureates

Another nation besides ourselves is going through a lot of change. Good luck, because it is made up of very talented people.

26.5.1996 Here are a few observations about a country I recently visited. I'll reveal the name at the end. So don't look if you want to play a guessing game!

Apart from Canada, this country has more companies quoted on the Nasdaq stock exchange in the US than any other foreign country. Its outstanding young entrepreneurs (usually in their thirties) focus first and foremost on cracking the American market and then almost as a cherry on the top selling into their own domestic market. Their dream is a successful IPO – initial public offering – in America, as a result of which they as the founders of the business will become overnight millionaires.

The industries in which they are involved are hi-tech, specifically software development, medical appliances, communication equipment, biotech and agritech. One of the most spectacular examples to date is a company which produces a laser which removes varicose veins from legs. The technology was adapted from an instrument that peels paint off jet aircraft. Having started with a few million rand several years ago, the market capitalisation of the company is now over R2 billion.

The country is wooing foreign investors with a Law for the Encouragement of Investments. It offers a cash grant equivalent to a third of the capital value of any project which is established there. Alternatively, you can choose a ten-year tax holiday. Intel, a highly respected American company that makes microprocessors, has already sunk R2 billion rand into the country and is about to invest another R4 billion. The workforce is unusually productive if properly managed. Better ideas of how to do the job are spontaneously raised by employees, some of which are world-beaters. In two of the largest industrial operations in the country – admittedly both capital-intensive – the average annual revenue per worker in one is R700 000 and in the other R1 million.

The country's GDP has grown at nearly 6 per cent per annum

during the last five years and is currently close to $80 billion. This puts the country at the lower end of developed country status with a per capita income of $14 500 (given a population of 5,5 million). Inflation has fallen from 445 per cent in 1984 to 8,1 per cent in 1995, though it could rise to 13 per cent this year.

Tourists numbering 2½ million visited the country last year – a record. All things being equal, the tourist industry is likely to be a major growth area in the future along with hi-tech. Despite being a small country where every part is reachable by car in four or five hours, an amazing diversity of terrain and vegetation exists – from lush plains to stark desert. Moreover, the country has some of the most significant archaeological sites in the world with ruins and relics dating from every millennium since 6000 BC. Its sacred places are familiar from infancy to people of every religious persuasion. On a visit to a seaside resort, our guide pointed out a man of some eighty years who was a past state president of the country and had won a Nobel prize for bio-chemistry. He was accompanied by no less than four other Nobel prizewinners in science. Where else in the world would one casually bump into five Nobel laureates in one spot?

Despite the constant presence of soldiers with guns, the atmosphere is relatively carefree. In the two major cities, the young throng the cafés around the clock. They have great *joie de vivre*. On Friday nights, however, the streets are deserted and it is almost impossible to find a restaurant that's open.

Humour abounds. In one restaurant, a waiter was upbraided by an angry customer whose arm he had jogged, thus spilling the drink over the customer's shirt. As he left after the wigging, the waiter muttered to us: "That customer must have had horrid parents!" If you want to listen to the finest music in the world, the country has a national philharmonic orchestra with few rivals anywhere.

Finally, an up-market suburb on the coast has been renamed "Ra'ananna-fontein" because so many of the best and the bright-est from Wits University live there. You must have guessed by now where I'm talking about. Israel, of course!

Cool Britannia

My, oh my, how much the Labour Party in Britain has altered its outlook!

21.6.1998 Cool Britannia. According to a *Financial Times* article, that's the latest catch phrase to emanate from Tony Blair and his Labour government. What surprises me is the underlying reason given by Tony et al for Britain becoming such a cool trendsetter. They cite the changing attitude of the average Brit-in-the-street towards venture capital, enterprise and entrepreneurship.

For me, this revelation says more about the distance travelled by the New Labour Party itself than by the country at large. The party has come a long way from its traditional, collectivist roots to arrive at the conclusion that entrepreneurs pursuing their own self-interest are part of the solution. The cloth cap of the worker seems to have been exchanged for the bowler hat of the city gent. As one prominent venture capitalist commented in the article: "It is fair to say this government was pretty agnostic about venture capital when it come to power. What is so encouraging is that it now sees it as a major factor in creating wealth and jobs."

It appears too that Gordon Brown, the Chancellor of the Exchequer, was impressed by a paper written by Californian economist Horace Brock entitled "How the nation that fired the most hired the most". Between 1980 and 1995, US companies shed 42 million jobs while creating 67 million – a net gain of 15 million jobs. Talk about the creative destruction of capitalism! During the same period, Europe managed a net gain of only 4 million jobs. The difference in performance can partially be explained by the fact that the US has for some time possessed vibrant capital markets which assist emerging businesses and hence employment. Europe on the other hand is still developing such structures.

But the crucial difference is mindset. Until recently, venture capital in Europe has been considered small beer. The general perception has been that it is a world inhabited by spivs on the one side who are after a quick buck and dotty professors on the other raising money for their latest attempt at producing a perpetual-motion engine.

138

In the US, by contrast, venture capital is big business. The asset allocation committees of the big insurance companies and pension funds routinely allow up to 5 per cent of their total funds to be set aside for venture capital. Moreover, they don't view this as a social responsibility exercise aimed at promoting employment opportunities among disadvantaged communities. They do it because there's an awful lot of money to be made in backing fledglings who have hot ideas but lack the funds to develop them into full-grown businesses. It's a case of the early bird catching the fattest worms.

But not just the financial institutions in America are in on the act. Microsoft and Intel – jointly nicknamed "Wintel" by their competitors – are plunging substantial sums of venture capital into first-time businesses established by computer geeks in their Silicon Valley garages. Wintel wants to invest in David *before* he slays Goliath.

We have a trio of national conferences coming up soon which should take note of these developments: the poverty summit under the auspices of the churches which will be seeking ways out of the poverty trap; a seminar organised by Omega Investment Research on alternative investment and sources of capital in an emerging market; and the job summit under the umbrella of the government, business and labour. The message to all three is: focus on creating a venture capital network as a means of escaping poverty.

The State We're In

But as Will Hutton reminds us, it will be some while before Britain gets out of the woods.

4.6.1995 Will Hutton, the economics editor of *The Guardian*, has written a book called *The State We're In*. It is a best seller in Britain because it has captured the widespread mood of national decay.

Hutton puts it as follows: "Above all, we live in a world of us and them. The sense of belonging to a successful national project has all but disappeared . . . The country is unevenly divided against itself, with an arrogant officer class apparently indifferent to the other ranks it commands. This privileged class is favoured with education, jobs, housing and pensions. At the other end . . . more people discover they are the new working poor, or live off the state in semipoverty. Their paths out of this situation are closing down as the world in which they are trapped becomes meaner, harder and more corrupting. In between there are growing numbers of people who are insecure, fearful for their jobs in an age of permanent 'downsizing', 'cost-cutting' and 'casualisation'; and ever more worried about their ability to maintain a decent standard of living."

Hutton uses this analysis to classify Britain as a 30-30-40 society. About 30 per cent of people are disadvantaged because they have no jobs or part-time work. Another 30 per cent are increasingly marginalised and insecure in poorly protected jobs that carry few benefits; and 40 per cent are privileged. He blames the Conservative Party, free-marketeers and the short-term outlook of the banks and the City of London for the mess. Yet one should question how far back Britain's decline can be traced. It certainly started before the election of Maggie Thatcher as Prime Minister. The pre-Thatcher Labour Government did not preside over golden eras of British nationhood. Indeed, apart from victory in two world wars, Britain's accomplishments in this century have not even closely matched those of the previous two centuries. America, Germany and Japan have well and truly overhauled Britain economically. France, Italy and Canada all now boast a higher per capita income.

I believe the turning point for Britain occurred during Queen Victoria's reign. Having made it to be the number one manufacturing nation on earth, Britain failed to nourish the roots of its success. If you examine the geniuses behind the Industrial Revolution in the latter half of the eighteenth century, the individuals involved came from neither upper class nor financial backgrounds. The inventors, mainly from Scotland, and the entrepreneurs, mainly from Yorkshire and Lancashire, were scientists and craftsmen of humble origin. They were good at making things and making money out of making things. It was an era when such activity was considered honourable.

By the midnineteenth century, Britain's success had bred a new generation with very different ambitions. The children of the mill-owners did not want to get their hands dirty so off they went to govern India and other parts of the British Empire. Those who stayed at home joined a civil service expanding to cope with the new-found complexity of administering the world's pre-eminent nation. Britain's manufacturing base meanwhile declined. Now Britain is meaner because it is an overhead-laden society running out of money and steam. Its malaise has nothing to do with the stinginess of the Tories; Labour will have to be just as sparing with the diminished resources available. It has nothing to do with a free-market philosophy which worked for Britain in the eighteenth century. And it has nothing to do with the way the City of London balances risk versus reward; that reflects prevailing economic conditions. It has everything to do with Britain once again elevating its entrepreneurs and craftsmen above its administrators.

If Britain is a 30-30-40 society, South Africa is around 50-30-20, using the same definitions. In order to shift the numbers to the right (the more privileged end of the spectrum), we have to dispense with administrators – not add to their numbers. We have to create our own version of the Industrial Revolution. Especially, we ought to respect the people who make things. Otherwise, we'll end up with an imposing superstructure on top of a nonexistent productive base – a *QE2* powered by a lawnmower engine.

The Tatler
Flip through this magazine and you realise that the upper class (Hutton's 40 per cent) is very much alive and well.

31.12.1995 Staying at a fine house in Mpumalanga Province a few weekends ago, I picked up a recent issue of *The Tatler*, England's quintessential magazine for socialites. I always turn to the pages with the photographs of the English upper class at play. Even though I knew nobody, I was not disappointed. Those snapped all looked as if they'd just walked off the set of *Four Weddings and a Funeral*.

The event captured on camera was a charity pyjama party at The Savoy. To quote *The Tatler*: "Guests wore the best of British nightwear: the crispest cotton jim-jams and the naughtiest nighties available . . . Not everyone was impressed, however. A disappointed septuagenarian was heard to complain: 'I've seen more bare flesh at a hunt ball,' as many opted for the slinky cover-up."

The party, nevertheless, had that hearty look about it which makes it a peculiarly English affair. One photograph showed four well-bred young faces with slightly supercilious smiles, peaking out from under a white eiderdown provided at the party. Those faces could only have emanated from a posh London suburb like Knightsbridge. A case of DODD – definitely our draw, dear. Whether it's chinless wonders or rakish wits; creamy debutantes with names like Portia, Victoria, Georgia and Lucinda; Viscounts or Viscountesses, The Hon. This or That: the fortunate ones are selected to grace the pages of *The Tatler*.

If you are not already in the English upper class, you seldom crack it by being successful and wealthy yourself. Try and you will be condemned as "nouveau riche". But if you are the son or daughter of a successful father and he puts you down at birth for the right school, you can through deft choice of friends be absorbed into the upper class. As long as the inheritance is not frittered away, grandchildren and great-grandchildren are assured of acceptance. The process cannot be hurried. It's a slow osmosis spanning generations. Accents have to mature. Money has to be of a certain vintage.

Foreigners tend to frown on the English system of class, but it is a lot less divisive than ethnicity and religious differences. Notable is the fact that political leanings are not class-bound. One would suppose that the upper and middle classes vote Conservative *en bloc*, whereas the working class vote Labour. However, not only are there numerous "leftie" earls, but the bulk of socialist leaders and thinkers hail from the middle class. Meanwhile *The Sun*, a right-wing tabloid prone to publishing blatantly patriotic headlines, is the most popular newspaper among the masses. In addition, the long stay in power of the Conservative Party owes much to its working-class support.

However desperate some intellectuals may be for a classless society, it will never evolve. Karl Marx was right. Class is a universal phenomenon. He knew that birds of a feather flock together: common interest binds them. Here in South Africa, class is probably the best way to break down the old barriers created by apartheid. Nothing wrong with that.

Let me end up with a typically English upper-class tale. A lady goes up to three schoolboys, one each from Harrow, Winchester and Eton. She asks for a chair. The Harrovian promises to fetch it (showy manners), the Wykehamist actually fetches it (trusty service) and the Etonian sits on it (aristocratic arrogance). I am proud to be a trusty servant!

British Monarchy
Even without Diana the Firm is still headline news and a huge tourist attraction.

4.12.1994 The visit by Princess Anne to South Africa last week is a reminder of the really beneficial side of the British monarchy. The Princess Royal has, in her low-key manner, played an invaluable role in promoting the cause of underprivileged children around the world. Specifically, she has attracted the warmest of praise from every quarter in discharging her responsibilities as Patron of the Save the Children Fund.

Walter Bagehot, Editor of *The Economist* from 1861 to 1877 but best known for his book *The English Constitution* published in 1867, made many telling comments on the role of the British monarchy. *The Economist* itself selected the following four among others in a recent edition discussing the monarchy:

"We must not let daylight in upon magic";

"A family on the throne is an interesting idea also. It brings down the pride of sovereignty to the level of petty life. No feeling could seem more childish than the enthusiasm of the English at the marriage of the Prince of Wales. They treated as a great political event, what, looked at as a matter of pure business, was very small indeed. But no feeling could be more like common human nature as it is, and as it is likely to be. The women – one half the human race at least – care fifty times more for a marriage than a ministry";

The monarch has "three rights – the right to be consulted, the right to encourage, the right to warn. And a King of great sense and sagacity would want no others"; and

"It is idle to expect an ordinary man born in the purple to have greater genius than an extraordinary man born out of the purple".

With wit and wisdom (but excusedly old-fashioned views about women) Bagehot more than a century ago captured the essence of the monarchy in a way that no modern commentator has. The first point about daylight's effect on magic presages what is occurring now as a result of the power of the media and the amount of money publishers are prepared to pay people to write books providing inside and intimate accounts of the lives of the famous. This is not going to change, but puts much more pressure on anybody holding high office in this day and age to lead a life beyond reproach. I say this because I doubt whether there would be any debate about the future of the British monarchy were the Prince and Princess of Wales still happily married.

The second point about the image of the family and the powerful effect it has on the citizenry at large is the reason why so much prose and film footage continues to be devoted to the ongoing relationships between the members of the Royal Family. Contrary to some commentators, I do not think the family's popularity has been dealt a mortal blow by recent events at all. The cast over time will change and the public's adulation will ebb and flow according to the character of the new "royals". But interest will never wane. In that sense, the magic will remain.

The third point about the monarch having certain rights but not overstepping them has been astutely followed by the present

144

one. With respect to "the right to encourage", it is a shame that all the excellent but relatively humdrum work that the Royal Family has done in the fields of welfare and community development is overshadowed by the endless chain of sensational disclosures.

Bagehot's fourth point, reminding us that the Royal Family are mere mortals, is one that should constantly be borne in mind, given the overhyped world we live in. We are dealing with ordinary folk who happen through birth to be placed in extraordinary circumstances. I believe that a partial cause of the present turbulence inside the Royal Family is the incredible strain that they are put under to behave like superstars. Media attention will never go away, but it must surely make sense to reduce the glitz and return to a balanced coverage which combines the ordinariness and the splendour of the royal lives.

Because of its quintessentially British nature, the Royal Family is a trump card in the pack of the tourist industry there.

Camelot
The national lottery bug has really struck Britain. I wonder if it will be the same here.

23.4.1995 26-47-49-43-35-38-28. That combination of numbers will be forever remembered by Mukhtar Mohidin, a 42-year-old factory worker in the north of England. He told a colleague: "I'm shattered. I can't sleep or think straight. I've never known anything like this. I've been chain-smoking since I heard I'd won." Shortly afterwards he went to visit relatives in India.

The setting for Mr Mohidin's change of fortune was the Ulster Folk and Transport Museum in Belfast, Northern Ireland. The exact time it took place was ten minutes to eight on the night of 10 December last year. Shortly before, the Belfast Chime and Handbell choir had given a tuneful rendition of their skills. Then Guinevere, the machine owned by Camelot who are the organisers of the British National Lottery, did her thing – producing a random sequence of winning numbers. The lottery ticket with

145

the entire sequence belonged to Mr Mohidin. He therefore won the National Lottery's jackpot worth £17,8 million. The price of a ticket is £1. No wonder he was shattered and chain-smoked.

However, other stories are not quite so happy. Ian Ward, a shop owner in Poole, Dorset, brought four cards home to enter the lottery – one to fill in himself and one each for his wife Chris and his daughters Rebecca and Lizzie. Late for work in the morning, he rushed out of their house and only picked up three tickets to submit for entry. He left Rebecca's behind. As Murphy's law would have it, the one he left behind produced five of the winning numbers, plus the bonus number (the last of the sequence). It would have earned Rebecca £219 000.

Mrs Ward's words were different to Mr Mohidin's. She said: "I am afraid I wasn't very pleasant to him. We've been married for 15 years and I wanted a divorce. I couldn't stop shouting. It would have paid off the mortgage, we could have gone to Switzerland for Christmas, and then invested the rest for the girls."

Another story is more comical than sad. On Saturday 1st April, Mike Evans, the owner of a wine bar in West Drayton, Middlesex, saw his winning numbers come up in the weekly lottery draw on television. He thought he had won £22 million. In fact his wife, Julie, had played a clever April Fool's joke on him. She filled in a ticket with the previous week's winning numbers, sent him out for a cup of tea just before the draw and put a video on of the previous week's live draw. She let him believe in his good luck for fifteen minutes. She was repaying him for all the practical jokes he'd played on her.

You can see that the National Lottery has certainly livened up life in Britain. Nearly 60 per cent of the adult population play the lottery every week, spending about £2 each. It's the highest percentage of regular players of any lottery launched in the past twenty years. It has surpassed the most optimistic of expectations in terms of money raised since its launch on 19 November 1994. The total so far is about £1 billion. Half of that has gone in prize money, and the other half – after deducting administration expenses – has gone to charities, the arts, sports, the national heritage and a special millennium fund to celebrate the year 2000. Who said the Brits weren't gamblers?

If the South African government approves the recently published recommendations of the Lotteries and Gambling Board, chaired by Professor Nic Wiehahn, we could have our own national lottery in the not too distant future. The proposed split of proceeds is similar to Britain's. Half will go in prizes. Of the other half – again after deducting expenses – 50 per cent will go to the RDP; 20 per cent to sports development; 20 per cent to charities; 5 per cent to the arts, culture and heritage and 5 per cent to miscellaneous causes. If Britain is anything to go by, the lottery here will be a smash hit. I'll certainly be buying a ticket each week for a minuscule chance of scooping the jackpot. Should my number come up, I'll tell you in this column what it's like to be a winner!

CJD

I wish we had given as much publicity to AIDS as Britain has given to CJD.

31.3.1996 Mad cow disease. The worst nightmare for yuppies with hypochondriacal tendencies. How many of them must be figuring out the number of hamburgers, cottage pies and spaghetti bolognaises they've consumed – ignorant of the risk – in the last ten years?

It's a story made from heaven for the media. First of all, it has a scientific foundation. We now know the real name is Bovine Spongiform Encephalopathy (BSE) and the human equivalent to which it is possibly linked is the almost unpronounceable Creutzfeldt-Jakob Disease (CJD). Furthermore, the current storm arises from the evidence that ten CJD sufferers in Britain – seven of them already dead – were exposed to BSE in the late 1980s.

Then there's the dimension of horror. Something close to CJD was first discovered among cannibals in New Guinea who ate the brains of their victims. The disease takes years to incubate, is invariably fatal and turns the brain into a sponge – along the way destroying equilibrium and causing blindness and deafness. There's no cure and no vaccine. Its progress is described as more ferocious than AIDS.

We have the element of surprise. I always thought of cattle as herbivores lazing in sunny fields, munching grass. But, until safeguards were introduced in 1989, British cattle were apparently fed the brains and spinal material of sheep and other cattle. Indeed, BSE is thought to have originated in cattle feed containing processed sheep remains which were infected with a similar fatal brain disease called scrapie. Then, just as we were heaving a sigh of relief that the problem was Britain's and not ours, we were told that South Africa is the "ashtray" for British beef. We import around 27 000 tons a year or 3 per cent of annual consumption. Yuppies here have to worry too.

Inevitably, there's humour: one British newspaper had the headline "Sunday roast turns into a hot potato". But there's also tragedy: many British farmers face destitution; and job losses are already occurring throughout the system that gets the beef from the hoof to the market. Finally, we have hysteria caused by uncertainty and modern methods of mass communication. Television networks repeatedly show the same stock footage of a cow on its knees in a paddock waving its head in a frenzied manner. Can't they find another cow?

For me, this whole drama has two disturbing aspects. The first is the absence of some crucial statistics. What percentage of the 11 million British cattle are estimated to have BSE at the moment and how does that compare with the last ten years? What is the trend of new cases of CJD over the same period? Do any other countries besides Britain have BSE-contaminated herds and how many cases of CJD do they have? How do countries which are thought to be BSE-free compare to Britain in terms of CJD incidence? Whilst the scientists do further research, let the public have as much data as is available now.

The second point specifically concerns the South African media. Contrast the headlines that BSE is attracting with the low-key coverage that far more serious health threats at present are getting. For example, a recent report not given enough prominence said that as many as two million South Africans may be HIV-positive now. Likewise, another stated that one person dies from TB every forty minutes in South Africa. Moreover, multidrugresistant strains and the growing HIV epidemic will increase the number of TB cases by 10 to 20 per cent next year. A third article alluded to the 8 000 malarial cases and 55 deaths from the disease so far this year. These facts should share the headlines.

Cornish Magic
I've always had a soft spot for the Cornish, but the surf could be better!

19.4.1998 The whole of Cornwall only merited six leaves of the Domesday book. William the Conqueror's scribes obviously didn't think much of it in 1086. But I've had an addiction for England's most south-westerly county ever since I first visited the place in April 1960. To be exact, it's a small segment of Cornwall that I am familiar with. It stretches along the north coast from Padstow, through the resorts of Rock and Polzeath and the fishing village of Port Isaac, to Tintagel.

During the sixties, the senior partner of my father's stock-broking firm kindly invited me to his holiday house in Polzeath. More important for a fifteen-year-old was his family of five daughters and one son. I'll never forget my introduction to the joys of surfing on a chilly spring afternoon in an ice-cold Atlantic. I used one of those old wooden belly-boards with a curved end and made a complete hash of catching the waves, either jumping too early or too late. However, one piece of advice the second daughter – Diana – gave me on that day has stood the test of time at Ramsgate in Natal and Fish Hoek in the Western Cape: double waves that almost break on top of each other give the best ride. I still possess a wooden board which is considered a bit of an oddity now on the beach.

Polzeath today is the surfing capital of England and boasts three surf shops fully equipped with the latest gear. The fact that even a big swell there is equivalent to a flat day in Durban or

Kommetjie does not deter the British surfing enthusiast. I counted over fifty in the water as a daily average during my short stay in September last year. They have to paddle a lot to get on a wave!

Port Isaac to the north is one of those seaside villages with impossibly steep and narrow streets down to a small quay where the boats are berthed. The roofs of the little cottages are stained with mustard-coloured lichen. Someone once said that Cornish fishermen only read two books – the Bible and the sea. In the Wrecker's Bar at one pub is a rhyme about one of the more dubious pursuits on the coast. It goes: "If you wake at midnight and hear a horse's feet, don't go drawing back the blind or looking in the street. Them that ask no questions seldom tell no lies, so watch the wall my darling as the gentlemen go by." This verse was referring to the smugglers who brought in "brandy for the parson and 'bacco for the clerk".

A little to the north lies another deserted village called Port Quin. The most frequently heard story is that the fishing fleet put out to sea as usual, was caught in a sudden storm and never returned. This tragedy is depicted in Frank Bramley's painting *The Hopeless Dawn* at the Tate Gallery. In it a young widow rests her head in the lap of an old woman who is gently comforting her after the awful news has been imparted.

Further up the coast is Tintagel, which has a sensational line of grey, craggy cliffs, including a massive block of rock that juts out into the sea as a separate island. Indeed the name is derived from the old Cornish word "tin" which means a fortress and "tagell" denoting a constriction or narrows, i.e. a neck of an island. Legend has it that Merlin, the magician, discovered the infant Arthur close by his cave on the island's beach. The great poet Tennyson's words rang in my ears as I surveyed King Arthur's seat: "But after tempest, when the long wave broke, all down the thundering shores of Bude and Bos, there came a day as still as heaven, and then they found a naked child upon the sands, of dark Tintagel by the Cornish sea; and that was Arthur; and they foster'd him till he by miracle was approven king."

The Cornish had a special moment in England's history – after the Romans left and before the French arrived. At least they produced one world-renowned individual: Arthur. His mystique remains.

Guy Fawkes

He wasn't such a bad fellow that he has to be burnt at the stake every year.

12.11.1995 On the night of 4 November, I took my family to a fireworks display at St David's Marist College, a Catholic school in Johannesburg. They probably decided to hold the event a day earlier than normal because 5 November was a Sunday.

It was a moonlit night with rain clouds occasionally obscuring the face of the moon. Whilst one might imagine that this would spoil the occasion because of the lack of true darkness, it actually improved the display by providing a dramatic backdrop. Two new dimensions to the celebration of Guy Fawkes day were the use of skydivers with flares as a prelude to the fireworks and the fact that children, along with the usual firecrackers and sparklers, had been given luminous green and red pipes. In the form of rods or rings, these flexible toys made the field look like a gigantic swarm of energetic fireflies as the children waved them to and fro or tossed them in the air.

The celebration of Guy Fawkes day interestingly draws its roots from East and West. The East is involved because fireworks are of ancient Chinese origin – naturally – because gunpowder was an invention from China too. The use of fireworks spread westwards during the Middle Ages, along with the development of military explosives. With the passage of time, the displays have become more elaborate as new chemicals are added by pyrotechnicians for colour and new methods of launching are discovered. For example, when I was a boy, rockets hissed upwards from bottles and left a sparky trail. Now one has a mortarlike device which goes "ke-dumph" as it dispatches its load into the night sky. After several seconds of silence, a loud explosion accompanied by a fiery shower of light is the satisfying result.

The Western connection is Guy Fawkes himself. It was coincidental that the location for the display we went to was a Catholic school because Fawkes, born into a prominent Yorkshire family in 1570, converted to Roman Catholicism as a young man. He served with distinction in the Spanish Army in the Netherlands from 1593 to 1604. He was then persuaded by Robert Catesby to return to England to join a small band of conspirators who had become incensed with the cruel treatment meted out to Roman Catholics by James I, King of England. Basically, the King oppressed them because they refused to acknowledge him as Head of the Church.

The Gunpowder Plot, which the conspirators hatched, consisted of blowing up the Houses of Parliament on 5 November 1605 during the ceremonial opening of a parliamentary session. In the confusion following the explosion, they intended to kill or carry off the members of the Royal Family and to install Arabella Stuart as queen. But it was too ambitious a plan and too many people were in the know. So Fawkes was caught red-handed in the underground vaults shortly after midnight on 4 November. He was waiting to light the fuse that led to a ton of gunpowder stored in at least twenty barrels. He was dragged off to the Royal Bedchamber where in response to the King querying his motive he is alleged to have said: "Desperate diseases need desperation remedies."

His co-conspirators were all tracked down. After a brief struggle with the sheriff's men, the plot's leader, Robert Catesby, was shot dead at Holbeache House near Dudley in Staffordshire. Fawkes himself was executed with the other conspirators on 31 January 1606, in the Palace Courtyard. Their heads were displayed to the public on spikes.

The following year, it was ordained that services of commemoration should be held in every parish church on 5 November. The anniversary is still with us, though no longer in a religious context. Today, Fawkes would be called either a freedom fighter or a terrorist, depending on your point of view. On the one hand, he was trying to end the reign of an extremely unreasonable and despotic king. But on the other hand, if the plot had succeeded, many innocent lives would have been lost. At St David's, they didn't have a bonfire with the effigy of Fawkes on top. I'm glad because I've always found the burning of the "guy" – his straw head lolling forward in the flames – a sad affair.

Dunblane

Unlike Fawkes, Hamilton was a totally evil guy. Moreover, unlike America, this incident has led to an immense tightening-up of firearm laws in the UK.

24.3.1996 With his bespectacled, bald head he bore an uncanny resemblance to the late British actor, Donald Pleasance. His eyes had that same glittery intensity that landed Pleasance so many of the leading villain roles in movies. But 43-year-old Thomas Hamilton was a real villain. On Wednesday, 13 March, he shot dead sixteen children and a teacher in a primary school gym in the Scottish town of Dunblane. Thirteen other children and two teachers were also wounded. A recent class photograph of the little boys and girls with their teacher – the kids smiling at the camera in that slightly forced way that five- and six-year-olds do – makes the act seem even more indescribably evil. "The slaughter of the innocents" was the way one observer put it. Society must feel cheated of retribution as Hamilton chose to end his own life immediately after the slaughter was over.

This frightful episode will once again focus attention on gun control and the criteria according to which licences to own firearms are issued. In Britain, the granting of licences at present is restricted mainly to enthusiasts who belong to the local rifle range, to farmers who wish to get rid of vermin and to sporting people who shoot grouse and other game. Hamilton was a gun enthusiast who obtained the legal right to own four guns. He had no criminal record, but evidence gleaned from his life over the last 22 years pointed to emotional instability and the possibility that he was a paedophile. After being sacked as a Boy Scout leader in 1974, he endeavoured to set up unofficial boys' clubs throughout Scotland. He never stopped nursing a grudge about the way he had been treated. He was that very dangerous phenomenon – an armed misfit.

But how does one introduce an effective vetting procedure with regard to the applicants for gun licences? How does one subsequently review the records of successful applicants to see whether they remain fit to own weapons that are capable of killing many people? Obviously, one can ensure that licences are never given to or are withdrawn from proven criminals. But Hamilton was a case of a festering psychopath who had never actually committed an offence. How can one minimise the odds of someone like him slipping through the net?

These questions are even more pertinent in a country like ours, where wider ownership of guns is at the moment permitted on the grounds of self-defence. Of course, lobbyists for a gun-free society will argue that the chances of a repetition of Dunblane here can be eliminated by a complete ban on guns outside the police force and the army. South African gun-owners will respond that such a move would largely be irrelevant since most violent crime arises from unlicensed, not licensed, firearms. Moreover, the widespread disarming of law-abiding members of the public will merely render them defenceless against ruthless criminals.

No easy answer exists, but there is a lesson in Dunblane for South Africa. One of the great curses of modern society is the number of guns available – licensed or unlicensed – to the general public. Mankind is no less violent than it ever was and we will always have social outcasts like Hamilton. While a complete prohibition of guns in the hands of the ordinary citizenry is unreasonable as well as impractical, legal ownership must be highly restricted. However, this can only come to pass when the public have sufficient faith in the ability of the police and the army to protect their lives and property.

In the days of the Wild West, Marshall Wyatt Earp managed to earn such a reputation. Because the townsfolk of Tombstone were confident that he and his deputies could run any outlaw out of town, they surrendered their Winchesters and Colt 45s. We are a long way from that in the present South Africa. For example, concomitant with restricted gun ownership, we would need comprehensive weapons searches and exceedingly tough penalties meted out to anyone caught in the possession of an unlicensed firearm. On the latter point, the maximum penalty for this is death in Malaysia and Singapore. They don't have a crime problem. Will we ever get that tough?

Kal
Kal is an example of what can be done when it has to be done.

16.4.1995 Western Australia is Harley Davidson country. I even learnt the correct spelling of the legendary motorbike from the tattooed back of a sunbather on Cottlesloe beach near Perth. As just one state of Australia, WA – as it's called – spans a larger land area than southern Africa up to Zaire. Yet it has a population of less than two million, equivalent to a middle-sized South African city.

It's not on account of its wide, endlessly straight roads that I dubbed WA with the name of a motorbike. It was an advertisement I saw pinned to the noticeboard in a "Kal" hotel foyer. "Kal" is short for Kalgoorlie, where most of the gold in Australia has been mined. The ad offered trips around the local mining sites on a Harley Davidson – plus sidecar in the event of more than one in the party. I was there for the annual Australian Gold Conference which I attended after "cracking a few tinnies and cab savs" at a "relly bash" in Perth (Australian for having some beer and red wine at a celebration with one's relatives).

Kalgoorlie is located nearly 600 kilometres east of Perth. Gold was accidentally discovered there in 1893 when three Irish prospectors, Patrick Hannan, Tom Flanagan and Daniel Shea, were travelling through the area on their way to explore claims somewhere else (Coolgardie). One of their horses lost a shoe so they camped in Kal. That night, they stumbled upon what was later to be known as the "Golden Mile". The discovery led to a gold rush that peaked in 1903. In that year, the gold produced was nearly 40 tons from ore grading an average of 41 grams a ton. During this period, Kal and the neighbouring town of Boulder grew to a combined population of 30 000 supporting 93 hotels and eight breweries.

Production thereafter declined as grade decreased with depth, but the revaluation of gold in 1932/33 revived Kal for nearly thirty years. From 1960, however, decline set in again and by 1975 virtually all operations had ceased. In the late 1970s a rise in price once more came to the rescue. This time, Kal's gold field was increasingly mined by open-pit methods which, together with more efficient metallurgical techniques to recover the gold, assured Kal's ascendancy again. A happy consequence is that Kal's population has risen back to 27 000.

What lessons can we in the South African mining industry learn from the history of Kal? Although we're much bigger – the Wits Basin has yielded a total of 43 000 tons of gold against 1 300 tons from Kal – we have to be as entrepreneurial as the Kal miners to keep our ore bodies economic. The Kal companies were faced with virtually zero reserves in the mid-1970s, but came up with innovations in production which suddenly offered a positive profit margin again. Sure, the gold price at over $600 an ounce gave them a temporary windfall in 1980 and the deposits they targeted were shallow (ours are all deep). Nevertheless, a status quo mentality would have meant an opportunity missed. I noticed when I drove around it that Kal is still streamlining itself. You don't get the impression that there are too many overheads weighing down the operations.

The other lesson I brought back is that to pay one's workforce well, the number of kilograms produced per employee is what counts. In Kal, each mining employee produces about 20 kilograms of gold per annum, worth R900 000. The average annual pay of these employees is around R135 000, which by Australian standards is a good whack. They're earning 15 per cent of what they produce. In South Africa, the number of annual kilograms per mining employee is about 1,5, worth R67 500. The average annual pay is around R11 400, which is low by the standards of commerce and industry here. Yet it represents almost 17 per cent of what each employee produces.

156

On the basis of pay as a proportion of output, Australia is a little lower than South Africa. Thus, to improve the living standards of our mine workers but still remain competitive with Australia, we simply have to increase productivity. That means more kilograms per employee. There is no other way.

Staircase to the Moon
If you want to be a world-class tourist resort, be different.

22.3.1998 Where in the world would you climb the staircase to the moon; see a reincarnation of Elvis Presley on the anniversary of his death; ride a camel called Markham with a flashing tail-light; and see a movie in the world's oldest picture gardens?

The answer is Broome, located on the shores of Roebuck Bay, 2 200 km north of Perth in Western Australia. The first phenomenon can be witnessed at low tide on the night of the full moon. Its reflection in pools of water on the bay's mudflats gives the illusion of a stairway leading up to the night sky. Broome is famed for its 10-metre tides which in places recede 12 km to expose mudflats and mangroves.

The Elvis sighting, with a little bit of poetic licence, occurred during the Shinju Matsuri or Festival of the Pearl. A procession of floats paraded down the high street led by a ceremonial paper dragon. In addition to a failed dinosaur catcher, the other eye-catching item was the rock 'n roll king's lookalike in a big black limo with the registration "1 ELVIS". The annual festival celebrates the fact that Broome was the pearling capital of the world in the early part of this century, producing 80 per cent of global output. The mother-of-pearl shell was the main source of income, being greatly sought after for the manufacture of buttons. The pearls themselves were regarded as a bonus.

In its heyday, nearly 400 pearling luggers operated from Broome employing 3 500 divers, among them Filipinos, Malays, Koepangers and Japanese. Chinese immigrants joined the influx as shopkeepers, and Chinatown is still the heart of the central business district today. A monument at the end of the main street reads: "A tribute to all those who sailed the sea and dived in search of pearl shell. Their endeavours and sacrifices layed the foundation of Broome, Australia's first multicultural town." Indeed, with its large Aboriginal population, Broome is the antithesis of "Omo-land" – the whiter-than-white country portrayed in *Beckett's Trek* on SABC.

Whilst the introduction of plastic buttons nearly dealt the pearling industry a mortal blow in the 1950s, it has been resurrected by the establishment of cultured pearl farms. Quality pearls are grown around beads surgically inserted in oysters fished from the sea. Tourism, however, is taking over as the main money-spinner and that's where Markham the camel comes in. My wife and her sister rode him in Lawrence-of-Arabia style down Cable Beach which stretches for over 20 km along the Indian Ocean. The taillight owes its presence to an unfortunate accident involving a taxi hitting the rear end of a camel after sunset. The taxi came off worst, but it was felt that in future the camel should be a protected species.

The architectural highlight of the town, now entered into the Australian Register of the National Estate, is the cream-coloured, corrugated-ironed Sun Pictures. Originally built in 1916 by pearling master Ted Hunter, it screened its first talkie, *Monte Carlo*, in 1933. It is literally a garden with palm trees and deck chairs and of course a large outdoor screen – much classier than a drive-in. Posters of classic Hollywood stars like Humphrey Bogart and James Dean adorn the entrance and, would you believe it, the loos are called Marilyn and Charlie.

The film screened the evening we went was the instantly forgettable *The Beautician and the Beast* with Timothy Dalton and Fran Drescher. Unforgettable, though, was the sudden appearance of a Qantas airliner a couple of hundred feet overhead about to land at the adjoining airport. The scream of the engines temporarily drowned out the soundtrack. Broome never runs out of surprises.

Teenage Suicides in Oz

The grass is not always greener on the other side.

3.3.1996 Peppermint Grove, Claremont and Dalkeith are the choicest suburbs of Perth in Western Australia. They adjoin the Swan River. The view from the tinted windows of the multi-storeyed mansions which overlook the river is stunning. Yachts ply their way to and fro under a cloudless blue sky, an occasional cruiser full of tourists chugs past towards the open sea. Pink hibiscus and white and yellow frangipani border lawns that are malachite green despite the drought. Not a burglar bar on a window is in sight and only the occasional wall shields a house-owner from the public.

Property values are amongst the highest in the world. Hyde Park in Johannesburg, Kloof in Durban and Bishopscourt in Cape Town do not come close to the riverside properties in Perth (or Sydney for that matter). So imagine my surprise and sadness when a local resident showing me over this veritable Garden of Eden casually remarked: "In the house over there, a teenager committed suicide two weeks ago. There have been several such cases in these suburbs in the recent past." According to one Australian newspaper report whilst I was there, Australia has the highest fifteen- to nineteen-year-old male suicide rate in the world. It is the leading cause of death among this age group in Australia.

I ask myself what on earth could cause Australian kids who enjoy just about the highest living standards in the world to behave in so aberrant and tragic a way. They are certainly not subjected to the same tensions experienced by South African kids. They live in a beautifully ordered world where the headline on the local TV station is the putting down of two stray dogs by the SPCA. Surely we should envy them, given the widely held perception that we spend every 24 hours sliding down the razor's edge of an uncertain, crime-ridden society.

The common factors linking young suicides as cited in the Australian article included binge drinking (despite an extremely tough law in Australia against drunken driving), breaking up with a girlfriend and copycatting the suicide of a friend. Perhaps one could add to the list neglect caused by both parents selfishly leading busy lives to the exclusion of their children. The boy comes home every afternoon and lets himself into an empty house. He sees his parents go out every evening to yet another important engagement on the social calendar. Alternatively, they're too tired to give him quality time. Gradually he builds up resentment which he successfully internalises from the family around him. So when he takes that last and irreversible step to capture their attention, it comes as a complete shock to them. Loneliness killed him. Regret forever accompanies them.

It is a salutary lesson for South Africa that as it rejoins the modern world and hopefully settles down to the task of becoming a prosperous nation like Australia, there is no Utopia on the other side. The problems change, they don't go away. Drugs, pornography, the lack of spiritual meaning in today's "anything goes" materialistic universe, indiscipline and bullying at school, the demon of alcohol, the breakdown of the family, the boredom of spoilt kids – all these and more are set to replace the concerns and neuroses of the Old South Africa.

Nevertheless we can be different to other countries in how we handle the difficulties encountered by our young people in growing up. We should not blindly accept the societal models on display in the rest of the world. We should learn from their mistakes and emulate some of their solutions. We owe it to the next generation of South Africans to give them a world in which they have an abiding sense of purpose. We want adolescents who never want to quit.

Waz and Bec

A delightful pair of young Australians stayed at our home for a while. They taught us to relax!

8.2.1998 Waz and Bec have a different outlook on life to me. But then we come from different generations.

The pattern for me started when I was five. At that tender age,

I was taken on regular Sunday excursions to my grandmother's bungalow at the end of a country lane in Surrey. The highlight of each visit was tea at four. Granny used to bring in a sumptuous spread consisting of sandwiches and buttered brown bread on the one hand, and marzipan and chocolate cakes on the other. I was forbidden to make inroads into the marzipan and cakes until I had at least settled for several sandwiches and slices of brown bread. This instilled in me the principle that pleasure has to be deferred in order for it to be truly enjoyed – my earliest brush with Calvinism, so to speak.

School reinforced the pattern. For example, you first had to be a fag who cleaned shoes before you were a prefect for whom shoes were cleaned. At the same time, I observed my father's lifestyle. He had by this time moved us to a house in Haslemere, Surrey, from which he commuted each day to London where he was a stockbroker. For most of the year, he would leave for work before the sun rose and arrive back after dark. At weekends, he would toil in the garden and greenhouse. His marzipan was a three-week holiday in Scotland in August when the two of us would slog through the heather to some desolate loch to fish for trout. Invariably, another member of the London Stock Exchange would already be there fishing from the other side. So much for solitude.

University was a confusing interlude. Contrary to the philosophy of jam tomorrow, no painful apprenticeship had to be served. From the very beginning, life was one continuous ball. However, as soon as I started looking for a job, the pattern resumed. Everyone made out that a career was a forty-year climb up the ladder, after which you could retire and do all the things you wanted to do but couldn't when you worked. Meanwhile, there was the business of getting married and having children and putting up with them until they became reasonable human beings. Each experience had to have a period of sacrifice and self-denial and misery before it became pleasurable. Even then, pleasure was accompanied by guilt. How can one be free of anxiety for any length of time?

Waz and Bec, or to use their formal Christian names, Warren and Rebecca, are two highly intelligent Australians in their mid-twenties who do not view life like a treadmill with moments of relief. Rather, it's a cruise punctuated by work. They arrived in South Africa a year ago and spent some months with us before travelling around the neighbouring states. Then they took "Peppi", their battered old VW Beetle which performs better on the downhill, and meandered through KZN and Lesotho to the Cape. Having worked for an interval in Fish Hoek, they plan to return to Perth in Western Australia to spend a month with their respective families before going walkabout in the north of that continent. They practise minimalist living to make the pennies go further. Yet they have all the joy of experiencing the world while they are still young.

They're not alone in seeking a new paradigm. Today, many twenty-somethings are choosing the same option. Like strolling players, they take their act to different towns and stay only long enough to amass the funds required for the next episode of their lives. Happiness is around every corner, not something to wait a long time for. Voltaire warned a long time ago: "In one half of our life we sacrifice our health in order to make money, in the other we sacrifice money to regain our health. And while we are doing so, health and life pass us by."

Waz and Bec are not about to fall into that trap. But many yuppie couples who work ninety-hour weeks and pass each other like ships in the night – exhausted and uncommunicative – are doing so right now.

MU50
Beware the new bacteria and viruses!

30.11.1997 Under a section entitled "Plagues in general" in my book *The High Road: Where are we now?* I referred to a specific dread of the global medical fraternity: "Bacteria have an extraordinary facility to adapt genetically to external threats by transferring genes both within and between species. It can only be a matter of time before the gene conferring Vancomycin resistance is passed on to staphylococcus aureus.

"This will be a major catastrophe. Before the advent of penicillin in the early 1940s, staphylococcus aureus was often fatal by causing pneumonia, pus in wounds, boils, etc. Certain of its strains are now resistant to all but one antibiotic – Vancomycin. Thus, the transfer of Vancomycin resistance would give these strains immunity against today's entire armoury of antibiotics. We would then wind the clock back to the pre-penicillin era."

Well, I've got news for you. Keiichi Hiramatsu, a bacteriologist at Juntendo University in Tokyo, has reported a strain which is resistant to Vancomycin, the antibiotic of last resort. The strain is called MU50. *The Economist* takes up the story: "A baby who had developed an infection in the wound left by an operation for a congenital heart condition was referred to Dr Hiramatsu when the infection failed to clear up. The tenacity of MU50 was shown by the fact that the abscess was discovered only when the boy's chest was opened up for a second operation several months after the first. To cure it, Dr Hiramatsu had to employ an antibiotic known as arbekacin, which is not licensed for use in Western countries."

While some form of medicine is around which can successfully combat MU50, the antibiotic arsenal is looking increasing bare. More worrying still is that Dr Hiramatsu sampled ten university hospitals across Japan and the new strain was present in six. The high prevalence is put down to the fact that these hospitals in particular do intricate surgery and use more antibiotics than ordinary hospitals as a result. Nevertheless, the strain was also picked up in the latter as well. The latest information is that it has crossed the Pacific into the US, where a middle-aged Michigan man has been confirmed as having contracted the new infection.

In a laboratory experiment in 1992, William Noble, of University College, London, successfully transferred a Vancomycin-resistant gene from an enterococcus bacterium to staphylococcus aureus. The resultant bug was even more resistant to Vancomycin than MU50. Even though he furthered the cause of science by showing that such a transfer was possible, he was roundly condemned in some quarters because of the risk of this superbug breaking out of the laboratory.

163

Meanwhile, a recent edition of *Science* reports that a network of 72 hospitals and medical clinics around the world has been formed to fight multidrugresistant bacteria. In many places in the US, resistance in pneumococcus, which causes pneumonia and middle-ear infections, has jumped from 10 per cent five years ago to 40 per cent today.

In South Africa, the growth of multidrugresistant TB and malaria is of particular concern. The cost of treating these is over ten times higher than the normal drug-susceptible strains. Moreover, in the case of TB, there is always a chance of an outbreak in the hospital where it is being treated.

As one doctor whom I quoted in my book put it: "We may be able to clobber the new strains with a new generation of antibiotics that are currently being developed, but one gets the distinct impression that the bugs are catching up with us." Africa in the twentieth century has been a fragile equilibrium between nature and science. Let's hope nature doesn't win in the 21st.

Heavenly Miss
Be ready for a visit from outer space!

16.6.1996 Interesting news has been emanating from Arizona's Steward Observatory. Timothy Spahr, a 26-year-old graduate student from the University of Florida, has been using the observatory to survey the skies for asteroids moving in the Earth's proximity. Three weeks ago, he took two photographs thirty minutes apart of a bright dot with a tail. A few nights later, he again photographed the object. This time the dot was double in size and had moved a considerable distance against the background of fixed stars. He was therefore delighted that he had discovered yet another asteroid. Moreover, it was a big one. But his excitement soon turned to shock and horror when he realised the significance of his calculations on the asteroid's movements. The vectors showed that it was apparently heading straight towards Earth.

His survey partner, Carl Hergenrother, a 23-year-old undergraduate at the University of Arizona, confirmed the discovery with a 230-cm telescope on a nearby peak. As Hergenrother told *Time* magazine: "It was scary, because there was the possibility that we were confirming the demise of some city somewhere, or some state or small country." Estimates of the impact included a terminal velocity for the asteroid of over 93 000 kilometres an hour and an explosion in the 3 000-to-12 000-megaton range. An equivalent result would be obtained if you took all US and Russian nuclear weapons and blew them up collectively at one site.

So what happened? We're still alive. The asteroid missed but only by 450 620 kilometres. In astronomical terms, *Time* calls that a hair's-breadth or more appropriately a "heavenly near-miss". As another astronomer noted: "It might be a useful point to make that this object was discovered only days before closest approach, so that if it had been on a collision course with Earth, we would not have had time to do anything much about it."

So what could you do even with proper notice of an asteroid on collision course with Earth? The answer in the past has been to launch missiles with conventional or nuclear warheads which would either make the asteroid shift course or destroy it. A more recent strategy is to fire a swarm of steel spheres – the size of cannonballs – at the asteroid. For all those with high school physics, the kinetic energy of the balls when stopped by the asteroid would be converted into heat energy. The heat would vaporise the asteroid.

This sounds like fairly puny research to pre-empt an event that could wipe out a significant portion of mankind. When you think of all the time and energy people invest in trying to blow each other up, it would seem more sensible to divert some of those resources into (1) early detection of incoming asteroids; and (2) a system to destroy them.

Don't think a collision never happens and that the possibility of one can be ignored. Scientists estimate that three asteroids with a diameter of one kilometre may collide with Earth within a period of one million years.

If an asteroid like this hits the land surface, the crater created by its impact would be about 13 kilometres across. Furthermore, there would be a considerable short-term disturbance to the global climate. A collision in the ocean would produce gigantic tsunami-type waves which would be catastrophic for cities close to the shore.

The cause for the extinction of the dinosaurs 65 million years ago is still being hotly debated. One theory is that an asteroid or comet of approximately 10-kilometre diameter struck Earth and precipitated the end of Jurassic Park. It would be ironic – given all our worries about everything else – if out of the blue we met the same fate!

Pocahontas

The first medal goes to Pocahontas for crowding so much into such a brief life. Incidentally, I would also award David Andrew Price a medal for the sheer irreverence of his piece.

30.7.1995 Occasionally I read a review of a film, a play or a book that is a work of art. In South African circles, Barry Ronge sometimes rates an alpha as do Gus Silber and Mary Jordan. But the review that has caused me to write this article was written by David Andrew Price in the Asian *Wall Street Journal*. It was about *Pocahontas*, a film currently on the circuit here.

Given my nature, what appeals to me is its sheer irreverence. To have a go at something as motherhood and apple pie as a Disney cartoon (or animated feature as they call it nowadays) is courageous indeed. He was among the 70 000 who saw the premiere at the Walt Disney Company facility.

In his words, "the film tells the love story of Captain John Smith and Pocahontas. Trouble is, Smith and Pocahontas were never romantically involved. That isn't surprising; when they knew each other in Virginia in the early 1600s, Pocahontas was 10 or 11. Years later, Pocahontas did marry an Englishman, but it wasn't Smith. We know Hollywood fudges true-life stories to make them more marketable. But will someone please explain why the tale of the 11-year-old girl who saved the first permanent English settlement in America is insufficiently commercial? Or why she is Disney material only if the studio makes her 10 years older, love-struck and stacked?"

Now I've always known, like Price, that movies often simplify the story. Remember those Second World War films of the 1950s when the film industry in Britain was at its peak. I watched them as a patriotic schoolboy. They always featured the same debonair actors playing British prisoners of war who successfully escaped

167

from German POW camps. But the person who really left an impression on me was the surly German guard from whose clutches these dashing fellows always escaped. He was played every time by the same actor. He must have made a lot of money out of being the archetypal "enemy" soldier with a guttural accent.

Yet that is exactly when art becomes dangerous and slips so easily into propaganda. Real life is complex and full of surprising contradictions. If art takes a real situation and smooths out the inconvenient edges for the observer, archetype can become stereotype, stereotype can become caricature and caricature can be downright misleading. Price, for example, points out that the ballad "Colors of the Wind" in *Pocahontas* implies that the Powhatans, the Indian tribe to which Pocahontas belonged, were antimaterialistic folk. But as he states: "Chief Powhatan collected steep taxes from the conquered peoples – 80 per cent of all that they grew, caught or created, from grain and fish to pelts and pearls . . . Also, the Powhatans traded avidly with the English for their goods." Not even South Africa has such a high rate of tax!

Price continues: "Viewed in the light of their times and backgrounds, stripped of cartoon mythology, Pocahontas and John Smith are all the more remarkable. Unlike most Englishmen of his day (and unlike Disney), Smith believed it was important to understand and deal with the Indians as they were, not as symbols of primitive evil or virtue . . . What makes the real Pocahontas intriguing is that she was a child of privilege in Powhatan society who took a humanitarian interest in the English, and among other deeds, served as a peacemaker and arranged for them to receive food so they could live. In a letter to Queen Anne in 1616, Smith recalled that Pocahontas had saved the colony from 'death, famine, and utter confusion'."

I am sure that a lot of people, adults and children, will enjoy *Pocahontas* and not give a fig that it doesn't accord with history. They will be pleased with the romantic images conjured up by the plot. They will leave the cinema with their expectations satisfied and their late twentieth-century notions of seventeenth-century Englishmen and American Indians suitably affirmed. Truth, though, can be stranger than fiction. Pocahontas subsequently married an English tobacco farmer called Rolfe. Together with her husband, she was received at the Court of James I in London in 1617. He was knighted and she became Lady Rebecca Rolfe. Shortly thereafter at the age of 22 she died of TB in Gravesend, Kent, and is buried at St George's Church there.

Leigh Armstrong
Leigh Armstrong gets a medal for educating me about the benefits of complementary therapies.

17.3.1996 "Leigh Armstrong. Reflexology: attain normal body harmony for perfect health. Aromatherapy: massage stress and all related ailments away with healing oils." These intriguing words were printed on a sandy-coloured business card dropped on my table at a breakfast organised by the Border Chamber of Commerce in East London. After the breakfast was over, the lady in question came up and introduced herself. Then ensued a fascinating conversation on "complementary therapies".

The basis of reflexology is as follows. Ancient cultures have mapped the body out on the feet in accordance with reflexes transmitted by the body's nervous system. According to the map, the body is divided down the centre. Each side is represented by the respective foot. For example, the heart and the spleen are located on the left foot and the liver on the right foot. The head and the brain are shared by the two large toes. The inner instep leading from the base of each large toe represents the spine. All other organs are equally divided between the two feet. By massaging the chosen areas on the feet, the reflexologist stimulates the body to heal itself through elimination of toxins, balancing meridians (the body's life forces) and relieving stress. The reflexologist will refer clients to other related therapists – homeopaths, naturopaths and chiropractors – as well as to doctors, where necessary.

Reflexology has risen to prominence in the West in this

century. However, in the East similar therapies based on meridians and pressure points have been administered for millennia – like shiatsu and acupuncture. That being the case, let us examine the major claims made by reflexologists on behalf of their profession.

* *Reflexologists can pick up health problems.* I have come across plenty of anecdotal evidence to support this contention. Heart, liver and kidney ailments as well as cancer, blood disorders and sinusitis have been identified in clients by reflexologists. The texture, sensitivity and colour of the feet provide telltale signs. People should still go to doctors for regular medical check-ups, but reflexologists may provide useful ancillary information.

* *Reflexologists can help to maintain good health.* Again, I don't think this claim can be disputed, because so many diseases today are psychologically induced or stress related. Although massage by a reflexologist can be very sore to begin with, touch in itself is therapeutic. Combined with a caring manner, it can rejuvenate a client. GPs have traditionally highlighted the importance of a "good bedside manner" for the same reason. I am sure, though, that doctors would maintain that reflexology is no substitute for vaccination against disease or for precautionary measures such as antimalarial drugs.

* *Reflexology can cure illness.* Being naturally sceptical, I find this the hardest assertion to accept. Personally, I would find it difficult to rely solely on the services of a reflexologist to cure me. It cannot be guaranteed that such therapy will strengthen my immune system to the point where allopathic treatment (eg: drugs, surgery) is not required. Nevertheless, I am prepared to accept that reflexology can substantially add to the beneficial impact of medicine and vice versa.

Having listened to Leigh, I would argue that now is the time to be open-minded and holistic. A society based exclusively on Western

170

medicine is as poorly served as a society which shuns it. The West and the East really do complement one another. Despite the incredible advances that have recently been made in medical science, much about the functioning of the body remains a mystery. Moreover, not only are bacteria and viruses finding chinks in the Western armour by developing resistant strains, but the costs of Western medicine are soaring. Surely it makes sense then to grant that reflexologists and other therapists should occupy a crucial niche in a country's health system.

Ian Woodall and Cathy O'Dowd

Despite all the controversy surrounding their ascent of Everest, you cannot take the honour of being the first South African team to reach the summit away from them. It requires a special kind of guts and commitment to do something like this.

9.6.1996 Congratulations to Ian Woodall, Cathy O'Dowd and the late Bruce Herrod for their magnificent achievement of climbing to the top of Everest. My wife and my daughter walked to Annapurna base camp in October 1994 and they were overcome by the awesome size of the Himalayas as well as the friendliness of the Sherpas. But the SA team's exhilaration at the summit must have been of a different order of magnitude.

To get some idea, I pulled out two books from our shelves at home – Chris Bonington's *Everest: The Hard Way* and Tim Macartney-Snape's *Everest from Sea to Summit*. The description of Doug Scott (one of Bonington's party) when he reached the top was as follows: "All the world lay before us. That summit was everything and more than a summit should be. My usually reticent partner (Dougal Haston) became expansive, his face broke out into a broad happy smile and we stood there hugging each other and thumping each other's backs. The implications of reaching the highest mountain in the world surely had some bearings on our feelings. I'm sure they did on mine, but I can't say that it was that strong. I can't say either that I felt any relief that the struggle was over. In fact, in some ways it seemed a shame that it was, for we had been fully programmed and now we had to switch off and go back into reverse. But not yet, for the view was so staggering, the disappearing sun so full of colour that the setting held us in awe. I was absorbed by the brown hills of Tibet. They only looked like hills from our lofty summit. They were really high mountains, some of them 24 000 feet high, but with hardly any snow to indicate their importance. I could see silver threads of rivers meandering down between them."

Haston wrote: "We were sampling a unique moment in our lives. Down and over into the brown plains of Tibet a purple shadow of Everest was projected for what must have been something like 200 miles. Slowly creeping into the euphoria came one very insistent thought as the sun finally won its race with the clouds and slid over the edge. The thought? Well, we were after all on the top of the world but it was still a long way back to Camp 6 and it was going to be dark very soon and then what would we do?" Scott and Haston both made it down.

Macartney-Snape in his book said: "Everest has a classic summit. It rises uncluttered by subsidiary bumps to a single, snowy apex. It is not exactly a pinnacle; three great ridges meet there to form a wind-rounded area the size of a large dining table. There is enough room for at least half a dozen climbers to sit on it uncrowded. When you climb onto it you have absolutely no doubt that you are on top of everything. Gazing out over mountains and cloud-filled valleys, with the deep blue dome of an endless sky above, you get an incomparable feeling of loftiness."

During Chris Bonington's 1976 expedition the photographer, Mick Burke, died. He was climbing alone behind two other members of the party (Pete Boardman and Pertemba) who ascended to the summit two days after Scott and Haston. In his case, his death was due to bad weather suddenly setting in. As Bonington, the expedition's leader, wrote: "I know that I and, I suspect, most other members of the team, would have followed the same course as Mick, in similar circumstances. In pressing on alone he took a climber's calculated risk. He balanced in his mind the risks of going on by himself in the face of deteriorating weather, with the knowledge that there were fixed ropes on all

172

the awkward sections. Sadly his calculations didn't work out. We were rather like the mourners after the funeral; glad to be alive, getting on with our own lives, the memory of Mick held with sadness and regret, yet accepted as an act that had happened; one of the risks of our climbing game. Is there a self-centred selfishness in this attitude? For those of us who are happily married and have children, there must be or we should not have carried on our life of climbing aware, as we are, of the risks involved. In our own single-minded drive and love for the mountains, we hope that the fatal accident will never happen to us, are frightened to contemplate the cruel long-lasting sorrow suffered by the widows, parents and children – an endless tunnel that for them must never seem to end."

Greenside High
This school gets a medal for being such a second family to the pupils.

20.10.1996 Valedictory assemblies for matric pupils are sweet and sad affairs. Sweet because the departing students have everything to look forward to in the world outside. Sad because an important phase of their lives has ended and friendships forged at school are never quite the same afterwards. I was privileged to be the guest speaker at this year's valedictory assembly at the Greenside High School in Johannesburg. James Small is a famous old boy. But apart from producing handsome and volatile rugby players, the school has an enviable academic record. This is exhibited by the numerous portraits in the entrance hall of students with five or six matric distinctions.

Despite having done my fair share of prize-giving ceremonies, I never tire of the look of unalloyed joy on the faces of the prize-winners as they walk up to the stage for their awards. It takes me back to the one and only time I ever approached the dais under such felicitous circumstances. It was at my preparatory school, Twyford, near Winchester, when I was twelve. I was awarded my soccer colours which consisted of receiving a dark blue tie with distinctive white stripes.

The moment was particularly exquisite since I was not a naturally gifted player and the prize was unexpected. In fact, a previous report of my sports master criticised my agility on the field – "He turns slower than milk," he said. However, as right half in a key 1st XI match, I had the good fortune to loft the ball from the halfway line over the opposing goalkeeper's head. He was way off his line at the time and the ball sailed smoothly into the top left-hand corner of the net. I can still replay the ball's fluky trajectory in my mind's eye, in super slow-mo and glorious technicolour. I wore the tie to a frazzle during my remaining primary school career. Whoever the stick-in-the-mud was that day who delivered the guest address must have also marvelled at the wide grin on my face. No achievement since then conjures up quite as golden a memory.

Returning to Greenside High, the departing head boy, Callen Hodgkiss, made a marvellous comment during his farewell speech. He congratulated the teachers "on getting up every morning to go to school". But Callen represents an example to us all. In Standard 6 he was knocked off his bicycle on his way to school by a taxi. For weeks he tenaciously clung to life before making a full recovery. Then he starred in every aspect of school life, for which at the ceremony he was awarded the most coveted blazer of all representing full colours in the academic, sport and cultural fields. The school rose as one to applaud him. Everyone admires pluck – that is why James Small is so popular.

Meanwhile, the departing head girl, Mandy Hinton, had to stop occasionally during her speech to compose herself. One could sense that she loved the school to bits. Every time she stopped, handkerchiefs would magically appear among the mothers in the front row to dab watery eyes. It made me think that parents really do entrust their children to the care of the principal and staff. If the school is exceptional, it becomes a second family with almost as strong emotional ties for the kids as genuine kith and kin.

What impressed me most about Greenside High was not its undoubted track record in the classroom and on the field. It was the humanity of the place. Would that all schools in South Africa were touched by the same compassionate and loving spirit!

Judie Lannon

Her work on postmodernism proved to be an outstanding contribution to our scenario team. She used the story of the Wizard of Oz to illustrate one of her points.

16.2.1997 One of the great benefits of doing long-term futures work is meeting some of the outstanding overseas minds in fields such as demography, technology and values. In the last category, much of the material on "postmodernism" contained in *The High Road: Where are we now?* comes from Judie Lannon, an American living in London. In the brilliant presentation she gave to our scenario workshop in Midhurst, Sussex, in September 1995, she identified "the Wizard of Oz revealed" as one of the major forces shaping the business environment in the 1990s.

For those who are too young to have seen the movie with Judy Garland playing a young girl, Dorothy, let me explain. Dorothy travels down the yellow brick road in her scarlet shoes to Emerald City with Tin Man, Scarecrow and Lion. They were off to see the great and powerful Wizard of Oz in order that Tin Man could acquire a heart, Scarecrow a brain and Lion courage. When they were ushered into the room and Dorothy presented the broomstick of the wicked Witch of the West to the Wizard, he boomed out some thunderous pronouncements from behind the curtain which made them quake and cower.

These pronouncements were accompanied by smoke and fire and terrible images of his face. Then Dorothy's dog, Toto, trotted forward and pulled back a curtain behind which the great and powerful Oz was concealed. This revealed a small, avuncular old man talking into a big megaphone. Dorothy was obviously very irritated and accused the Wizard of being a very bad man; to which the Wizard replied: "Oh no, my dear, I'm a very good man. I'm just a very bad Wizard!" Alas, his mystery was forever destroyed.

This kind of revelation is occurring every day in the world, given the power and universality of the modern media. CNN's star correspondent, Christiane Amanpour, last year graced the cover of *Newsweek* as the first lady of global TV. Some reporters are now greater celebrities than the people they interview. The transfer of authority from traditional authorities to "media power" is the source of much of our moral and ethical confusion. Politicians, the judiciary, huge corporations and even Prince Charles have gone through the experience of the Wizard of Oz. The magic disappears. It is no coincidence that ex-leaders of several countries and many captains of industry have been exposed, arrested and put on trial for corruption.

Another bright lady teaching at St Mary's DSG in Kloof pointed out to me a second, and in many ways a more poignant, message from the film *The Wizard of Oz*. After being revealed, the Wizard went on to show that Tin Man, Scarecrow and Lion had indeed acquired the qualities which they desired on their way to see him. They didn't need a wizard to wave a wand. They inadvertently did it for themselves. When I wrote *Pretoria will Provide and Other Myths*, the myth in the title makes the same point. The state is no longer a wizard with magical powers. The best that the state can do is provide an enabling environment in which people meet their own goals along the way.

So the story of *The Wizard of Oz* ends on an upbeat note. It suggests what amazing inward powers we as individuals have to transform our prospects. We don't need wizards because we have more control than we think over our future destiny. External agencies can merely provide a following wind.

Tony Blair

I have to hand Tony Blair a medal for maintaining such an incredibly high popularity rating among the British population. He is a passionate leader with a clear sense of direction.

18.5.1997 It's worth repeating the recent UK election result to show how remarkable it was – the worst drubbing of the Conservative Party since 1832. Labour 419 seats (273 held, 146 gained), Conservatives 165 seats (165 held, 178 lost), Liberal Democrats 46 seats (18 held, 30 gained, 2 lost) and Others 29.

Notice no seats lost by Labour, not one gained by the Conservatives. The share of the vote was Labour 45 per cent, Conservatives 31 per cent and Lib-Dems 17 per cent, the swing from the Conservatives to Labour being 10,2 per cent. One of the wonders of the first-past-the-post constituency-based system is that a 10 per cent swing can cause such a huge transfer of seats. But there it is.

Simply put, Britain wanted a change of government after eighteen years of Conservative Party power. The clean-cut, morally zealous, photogenic Tony Blair, together with his super-achieving wife, Cherie, and model family struck exactly the right chord in the hearts and minds of the British electorate. Their youthful freshness contrasted sharply with the image of sleaze, staleness and disunity over Europe that hung around the Conservatives. So it was no contest! Paddy Ashdown, leader of the Lib-Dems, was no slouch either in showing up the Conservatives. He must have been pleased with his 46 seats.

However, the result ran completely contrary to one theory of the pundits summed up in the phrase, "It's all about the economy, stupid". If that were the case, John Major would have walked it. Britain really has never had it so good since the Second World War. No more the sick man of Europe, the country's economic growth is respectable and unemployment is down. Why didn't this count?

I think Will Hutton in his best seller *The State We're In* puts his finger on it. A large section of the British population simply don't believe they're participating in the new-found prosperity. Indeed, statistics show a widening gap between rich and poor. Blair, with his compassion, made the marginalised people feel part of his flock. But, like a smooth minister in the pulpit, he offered salvation without pain – pennies from heaven – and therein lies the danger. It is precisely because Britain suffered pain in the Thatcher years that it is in such a competitive position today. The rules of the economic game give the new Labour party very little room to manoeuvre in its quest to improve the social conditions of the country. Spend more by raising taxes and you discourage investment. Raise the unit cost of labour by legislating for better employment conditions and you become less competitive. Britain's new rulers are hemmed in by global forces outside their control.

It will also be interesting to see whether Blair has the strength of character of a Paul Keating (the former Prime Minister of Australia) to keep the extreme Left in his party under check. Keating, you will remember, made himself pretty unpopular with his statement that Australia would degenerate into a banana republic if it didn't mend its ways. Blair, on the other hand, is inheriting a going concern where many of the tough reforms have already taken place. Because of the absence of a crisis, he may be tempted to let up. When Blair addressed a business audience in the city of London before the election, he wowed them so much that one of them asked: "Is there anyone else in the party like you?" The question was based on the suspicion that many of Blair's backbenchers have a natural antipathy towards business.

Time will tell whether these doubts have any foundation; or whether Blair will be a radical prime minister who effectively creates a more inclusive society and thereby enhances the economy. But I've left the best remark about the election till last: "Blair would have won the election whichever party he led." It reveals two things. Blair's policies aren't that different to the others: Thatcher left her footprint. And when you're 43 and the youngest Prime Minister of the century, you're capable of anything. Good luck to him!

Princess Diana

This article demonstrates the devastation that I feel in awarding this medal posthumously. The only fact that may be wrong after the lengthy inquiry in France is the speed at which the Mercedes was travelling when it hit the pillar. But drink and drive appears at this stage to have claimed the lives of Di and Dodi and their chauffeur.

7.9.1997 Some moments are on record forever. The last time, a wintry night in November 1963. Walking down the steps outside the library at New College, Oxford. Someone whispers, "JFK's been assassinated". Exact memory of place and time. Everyone has.

Bright sunny Sunday in Perth, Western Australia. Arriving for lunch with friends in the suburb of Duncraig. Getting out of car, shaking hands, then host saying: "Princess Di's been killed in a car crash with Dodi and his chauffeur. Her bodyguard is critical." Sun warm on my back. Real world. Total disbelief.

Walk inside. Television on. CNN anchorman teary-eyed and grim. Headlines to confirm news at the bottom of the screen. Glimpses of wreckage in lit-up tunnel. Night-time so far away in Paris. Curious onlookers peering over the parapet. This is how the BBC announced it. National Anthem, Union Jack waving in the wind. Like candles in the wind – they've been snuffed out.

Monday on plane to England. Di's new love featured in previous week's journals. Articles out of date. Suddenly, no longer relevant.

Tuesday morning. Story begins to take shape in British newspapers. Decoy vehicle, then second driver puts pedal to the floor to outrace paparazzi. Drink and drive claims more victims. Speedometer frozen at just under 200 kilometres an hour. No wonder Mercedes looked as if a train had hit it.

Meanwhile, hot, muggy, September day in London. Thames climate. Walked to Buckingham Palace. Flowers and messages everywhere in front of the palace. Queen of Hearts, the Jewel in the Crown, People's Princess repeated again and again. Huge collection of media to the left of palace. Satellite dishes, vans, video cameras waiting for what? Diana's no longer here.

Then to St James's Palace. Queues of people waiting up to eight hours to sign the Book of Condolence. Shuffling forward silently. Walk on to Kensington Gardens. Despite approaching autumn, trees and flowers are in brilliant colour. The front of the palace is the epicentre of mourning, as it was her home. Thousands upon thousands of flowers arranged neatly in a semicircle outside the gate. Flowers and messages taped to the railings. Left my own. Hope William and Harry follow in her magical footsteps. People arriving from all over the park – old, young, toddlers – carrying more flowers. Police directing the flow in and out of the Gardens. Never anything like this before. Diana's popularity utterly over-whelming. Only now apparent. Two young mothers picnicking on grass feeding babies with bottles. Life goes on.

Pictures in a Notting Hill Gate café showing Diana winning a mother's race and white water rafting with her two sons. Every-one laughing in the raft. Diana so alive, now dead. One of a kind, who went way beyond the call of duty to help those less fortunate than herself. So human, so approachable, yet so incredibly beautiful. Her talent to bring a shining light into people's lives was God-given. Now God has taken her away. Adieu.

The Bride
Any dad will award his daughter a gold medal for the way she looked on her wedding day.

15.9.1996 *Father of the Bride!* Have you seen the movie? Well, I have. What's more, I am going to go through the actual ex-perience for the first time this coming Saturday. By the time you read this article, the ceremony will be over, my daughter, Katy, will be launched into marriage and I will be in a recovery mode. It makes a big difference if you like the guy your daughter is marrying and I really do. This, despite the fact that we played golf last weekend and he beat me by sinking a three-foot putt on the eighteenth green!

My mental state leading up to this marriage is well illustrated by an experience I had at a Johannesburg restaurant last week. I took out my mother, who has come from England for the wed-ding, for lunch at the French Bistro in Rosebank. At the end the bill was R140. Because the service and the food were excellent, I added another R20 for the tip. As I walked out of the restaurant the lady behind the till beckoned me towards her. She whispered that I must have over-tipped the staff. Indeed I had: I had given her R260 instead of R160. So she handed me back a R100 note. I thanked her profusely and excused my temporary lapse of arithmetic competence on the grounds of premarital parental stress. How many restaurants in South Africa are as honest as the French Bistro!

Three scenes from the aforementioned Steve Martin movie have resonated in my mind during the frenetic countdown over the past few weeks. The first was when he was given an estimate of the cost of the wedding by Frank, the wedding co-ordinator. His response was: "Whew, that is more than our first house!" For me, the South African inflation rate over the last twenty years has easily accomplished the same result. I once heard that the road signs erected not so long ago on the Ben Schoeman motorway linking Johannesburg with Pretoria cost more than the original motorway. Hence, I am not surprised that my wallet is a lot thinner.

The second scene was where the bride's father tries on the tuxedo that he wore at his own wedding and dances around the room to the sounds of "What's New Pussycat?" – an old melody of Tom Jones. For a moment, I though he'd got away with it although his artificially created hourglass waist reminded me of a Victorian lady severely confined by a tight corset. However, the inevitable happened. Subsequent to his athletic twirls, he bent forward ever so slightly, the seams couldn't take it and the jacket promptly split wide open at the back!

With that scenario in mind, I went to Hawes and Curtis, a men's outfitters close to Anglo's Head Office in Fox Street and ordered a new dinner suit. Thanks to the mild-mannered and highly skilled tailor, Mr James, I shall trip the light fantastic when the disk jockey plays the golden oldies without a care in the world. I have especially requested "Do You Love Me?" by Brian Poole and The Tremeloes to test the limit of the dancing prowess of the wrinkly contingent.

The third memorable scene of the movie is yet to come as I write. At the wedding itself, the bride's father goes through the excruciating experience of arriving several seconds late for each major event and therefore misses things like the cutting of the cake and the departure of the newly married couple. He never quite succeeds in catching up with the schedule. I am determined to be there every step of the way, physically as well as spiritually, and enjoy every minute.

Actually, that is being selfish. If, at the end of the day, my daughter and son-in-law have as much fun as my wife and I did at our wedding on a small farm outside Pretoria, it will all have been worth it. I remember our jaws ached from perpetually smiling for all the guests. One of them hid bacon in our Mini's engine, which created a terrible pong the following day as we drove to Durban. I also recall a humorous remark from a friend at the time: "Marriage rests on incompatibility – where one partner has the income and the other the patibility." I have slightly amended his quotation on the grounds that you never know which gender plays which role these days. Nevertheless, Mendelssohn's Wedding March will stay the same!

Howard Angus and Richard Noble

I am awarding medals to two of my high school compatriots who both feature in The Guinness Book of Records.

16.11.1997 I was thumbing through some old photographs the other day when I came across a black-and-white one of my high school compatriots at Winchester College. I boarded in a house called "Freddies", and this was the annual house snapshot where we were formally dressed in dark suits, white shirts and quiet ties. We were 44 young guys with our future ahead of us. The year was 1960.

I wonder where my colleagues are now, since I lost contact with them when I came to Africa eleven years later. I'm sure most of them are teachers, preachers, brigadiers, lawyers and civil servants because that is what the place produced. John Betjeman, the poet, wrote the following about us: "Broad of Church and broad of mind, broad before and broad behind; a keen ecclesiologist, a rather dirty Wykehamist." The last-mentioned term is derived from the fact that William of Wykeham founded our school.

Serendipitously, one of the 44 pitched up in South Africa

recently and has settled down here. So we play the occasional game of golf together and swop the usual yarns. This year we had an Old Wykehamist dinner at the Inanda Club in Johannesburg. Five "Old Woks" from various eras mustered there with their respective wives and girlfriends. This was enough to hold a "hot", which is Wykehamical slang for a scrum, after the meal was over. Alas, the youngest member of our fivesome broke a rib during this ceremonial horseplay. He has since recovered.

Freddies hasn't produced many famous people. However, the photograph is singular because it contains two people who have featured in *The Guinness Book of Records*. One is Howard Angus whom I partnered in the school's first pair at rackets. This is a very fast form of squash played in a court four times the usual size with something resembling a golf ball. But it was at another sport he excelled. He won the real tennis amateur championship of the British Isles no less than sixteen times between 1966 and 1980 and again in 1982. He was also the first British amateur to win a world title in 1975. Real tennis is not to be confused with lawn tennis which was developed from it in the 1870s.

The second person made headlines in the newspapers a few weeks ago. I remember him as the lead guitar in a house rock group and tinkering endlessly with diesel engines which powered model cars and aeroplanes. In my photograph he is sitting cross-legged in the front row with a shock of black hair. Age has made his face rounder and his hair sparser and greyer. But the eyes have the same intensity.

His name is Richard Noble and from 1983 to 1997 he was the world land speed record holder at 1 019 km/h. He wasn't upset at losing his record since he was the manager of the team that broke it on 15 October at Black Rock in Nevada in the US. In Thrust SSC, Andy Green – an unflappable fighter pilot in the Royal Air Force – broke the sound barrier with an average speed of 1 228 km/h over two runs in opposing directions. Everyone agrees that, but for Noble's energy and enthusiasm, the project might well have faltered. As he said afterwards: "For the first time in six long years I can sleep easy and take the family on holiday. The project has achieved every objective we set."

It's nice to have been at school with two people who in quite different sports have undoubtedly proved that they are world class.

Isaiah Berlin

Isaiah's philosophy is very pertinent to the South African situation, because we still believe in big solutions to our problems. Actually, it will be about getting lots of little things right.

23.11.1997 Isaiah Berlin, whom I rate as one of the great British philosophers of the twentieth century along with Alfred Ayer, Bertrand Russell and Gilbert Ryle, died this month at the age of 88. Winston Churchill once invited Berlin to lunch at 10 Downing Street and asked him what his best philosophical piece was. "White Christmas," was the puzzled response. Somehow Churchill had managed to confuse Isaiah with the other Berlin who was famous at the time – Irving – and had sent the invitation to the latter!

In fact, the best piece I remember of Isaiah's was *The Hedgehog and the Fox*. In it he wrote: "There is a line among the fragments of the Greek poet Archilocus which says: 'The fox knows many things but the hedgehog knows one big thing.' " Basically Berlin divided the world into two kinds of people: hedgehogs like Plato and Dante who search for a single, overarching truth which ultimately ties everything together; and foxes like Aristotle and Shakespeare who accept life at face value, in other words, a tapestry of amazing diversity.

Berlin plumped himself firmly in the fox camp. To him "the pursuit of harmony is a fallacy, and sometimes a fatal one". Demanding subservience from the population to some grand, abstract idea represents "the victimisation of the present for the sake of an unknowable future". Life in reality is a constant trade-off between competing values. Push for absolute freedom and you sacrifice equality, but go for absolute equality and you diminish freedom. Be just and it's almost certain to be incompatible with mercy, but be merciful and you're bound to end up bending justice. In a good society, therefore, tolerance and compromise are essential qualities in order to overcome the inevitable clashes between multiple perspectives.

Berlin's spirit hung over a dinner I attended the other night when the conversation turned to the thorny issue of security booms in Johannesburg suburbs. One individual at the table contended that the community had every right to have them installed for their own safety, while another retorted that they transgressed the public's right of unimpeded access through the suburb.

A third member of the party intervened. He asserted that neither right was fundamental, so the situation should be judged on practicalities. He went on to say that two types of democracy existed – the one where people use a ballot box every five years and the other where they vote with their money and their feet every day. If the local authorities removed the booms in a heavy-handed way, the second type of democracy would apply and some residents would "semigrate" to Cape Town or emigrate overseas. This would endanger the Gauteng rate-paying base which was bad for everybody. So why not allow the booms to remain until the new initiatives by the SAPS had begun to reduce violent crime, whereupon a request to have them removed would be made? What a foxy answer worthy not only of Solomon but also of Isaiah.

In South Africa, we have plenty of elite hedgehogs who believe that big solutions to our problems are both possible and desirable. Personally, I'm a fox who supports the idea of getting lots of little things right so that the big things look after themselves.

Albert Mathibe

If only every single poverty-stricken community in this country had its own version of Albert Mathibe, we would be making huge inroads into the problem of poverty.

14.12.1997 Dynamite, they say, comes in small packages. Such is the case with Albert Mathibe who lives in, to quote him, "the ruralest of the rural, the dustiest of the dusty, the poorest of the poor" villages in the Northern Province. "We haven't yet produced an Isaac Newton, a Mother Teresa or a Nelson Mandela." The place he speaks of is Patantswana, near Nebo. Its income is mainly derived from the sales of surplus produce and from jobs in towns as far afield as Nelspruit. There is no signpost off the main road indicating Patantswana. It just says "to the mountains" and off you set down a dirt road that becomes impassable at times during the wet seasons. Luckily, it was okay for the opening of a new maternity wing in the village's clinic which I and three of my Anglo colleagues attended recently.

Albert started school at the age of fifteen and worked at the same time to pay for his education. Subsequently, he completed a teacher training course in 1975 and rose through the ranks to become principal of a local primary school. In 1990, he was sponsored to go to America to do a community development course at the University of Michigan. When he returned, he was determined to plough back all that he had learned into the community.

Were it not for Albert, the rural settlement of Patantswana would be just another desperate patchwork of subsistence plots. But his vision and drive, together with his ability to twist fundraisers' arms (like ours), have given Patantswana a first-rate community centre which includes the clinic, a community library and a pre-school/daycare centre. Much of the construction was carried out voluntarily by the villagers themselves.

Ominously, the proceedings to launch the maternity clinic started one hour behind schedule. This was due to the late arrival of the bus carrying members of the St Engenas Brass Band from the Zion Christian Church. My anxiety over the length of the programme was obviously tangible because the daughter of the contractor who built the new wing turned to me as we seated ourselves and said "it is never as bad in the real world as it is on paper".

And neither was it. The whole thing went like clockwork with the band playing and the choir singing between the speeches of the dignitaries. We recovered time lost and ended smack on lunchtime. The highlight of the day was a play on health care put on by the local schoolchildren that convincingly outshone *Sarafina 2*. The articulate way the kids got the message across underlined the value of the little library in the village. Placards with slogans like "Prevention is better than cure", "One love one partner", "No condom, no sex", "TB is curable" and "AIDS is incurable" hit home hard.

Uniformly, the speakers praised Albert for his contribution. After we unveiled the plaque, Albert proudly took us on a tour of the rooms inside. He then led me outside and showed me an area where the drainage system was deficient. "Perhaps you can finance this as well, Clem." My slight look of donor fatigue prompted him to add: "It never stops, you know!" and we both grinned.

In one respect, Albert was wrong in his appraisal of Patantswana. It has produced a champion – him. If only all rural settlements in South Africa could have someone like Albert, we'd be on the "High Road" for sure. He will never suffer from the local curse which goes: "Anyone who does not dream must not sleep." He can sleep soundly!

Mama

It is really worth visiting Mama's restaurant, if only to bask in her warm hospitality and read the pithy comments on the menu.

28.12.1997 Some days you strike it real lucky. I've been driving down to Selborne on KZN's south coast and I've just turned off the N2 highway at Park Rynie and then right towards Pennington. As I hit Kelso, I see this intriguing signboard with red and blue writing on a pale green background. It says "Mama's T Garden and Family Restaurant". I turn left up a road that hasn't been resurfaced since the Great Trek, follow further "Mama's" signs up a steep hill and arrive.

There are three paths into Mama's designated "young and adventurous", "mature and cautious" and "giants". I select the middle one even though I'm six foot four and therefore have to bow my head under an arch to gain entry. I walk onto a wooden deck, perched on stilts like a lookout post, overlooking miles and miles of shoreline. The view is stupendous, the best of any restaurant north or south of Durban. Lush vegetation below Mama's blots out the main south coast railway line running adjacent to the beach. Tall firs stand like sentries among the houses of Pennington. A vertical plume of smoke issues from a sugar mill in the distance. The sea's perpetual roar mingles with bird and insect sounds.

A young man ushers me to a shaded area of the deck and I'm now seated on a black wooden bench at a black wooden table, sipping tea. Red-chequered cushions soften the seat. A bell with a scarlet tassel (for service if the family is watching TV in the house), a colourful fibreglass parrot on a perch and a bunch of ripening bananas hang from the roof. A stone raccoon rests on my table. Ferns and other plants convert the deck into a shrubbery of its own. Oscar, a grizzled old Staffordshire bull terrier, pads up to sniff me.

At last, Mama comes out to greet me. She looks exactly like I pictured her from the sign – warm and huggable. She speaks in heavily accented English: "There are no sour faces here." Her name is Dana du Preez, a Czech married to an Afrikaans engineer. She and her husband plus their two kids, Nicholas (22) and Belinda (20), live on the property. Nicholas, who saw me in, now runs the business "as Papa wanted to give him something to do". She opened the restaurant in 1990 with two tables and her own tea set and cutlery.

Though I'm not staying for dinner, I flick through the menu. One item immediately catches my eye: Bavarian Oinck (smoked pork spare ribs) as a main course. Sprinkled between the dishes are some homespun philosophies. "The government deficit is the difference between their spending and the money they have the nerve to collect"; "common sense is special, not common"; "all secrets are alike – in one ear and out into another"; and "overweight is hereditary. It shows up in your jeans". Inside the restaurant, I see a bookcase with a complete set of *Encyclopedia Britannica*. Unusual!

As I leave, I throw a coin into a wishing well – a donation for the association of the disabled. Behind me, I hear: "Mama ensures that all your wishes come true." She waves me goodbye from the little piece of heaven on earth. I remember one last saying in the menu: "Live each day as if it were your last. One day you'll be right." Ah, well.

Pierre Wack
Pierre was my scenario planning mentor.

18.1.1998 A dear friend of mine died in the week of Christmas. His name was Pierre Wack. He was also the greatest scenario planner in the world.

With his goatee beard and his hooded eyes, one could easily mistake him for a monk devoted to some Eastern religion. This was not far off the mark. He loved Japan and had a Japanese wife. He also waved lighted joss sticks under his nose if he really wanted to concentrate. But his mannerisms gave away his Gallic roots. He would mysteriously pass his hand in front of his face when referring to a person's "microcosm" – his inner mindset. He would give an exaggerated shrug that only a Frenchman is capable of when presented with a "poorly observed fact". His accent was pure Aznavour.

I first met Pierre at the end of 1982 when he was about to retire from Shell as head of its scenario planning unit. He delivered a bewitching lecture to Anglo in Johannesburg on the perils of forecasting and the need to portray the future as an array of possible pathways, any of which could materialise. For the next ten years he was a consultant to us along with his colleague, Ted Newland. He introduced us to his "circle of remarkable people", all of whom were international experts in demographic, technological, social or political trends. He was a key player in formulating the global scenarios which formed the backdrop to our original presentation entitled *The World and South Africa in the 1990s*.

Pierre learnt his craft from the great American, Herman Kahn, in the 1960s. The latter wrote scenarios for the US Air Force which were immortalised in the book: *On Thermonuclear War: Thinking about the Unthinkable*. When Pierre joined Shell, he vowed to adapt Kahn's methodology to the world of oil and thereby make Shell a more flexible and learning-oriented organisation. His first set of scenarios fell on deaf ears because the idiom wasn't right for Shell management. He would remind me of this experience again and again. "Language is as important as content, Clem. A scenario that has no chance of changing the course of decision-making is useless even if it has been perfectly researched and turns out to be correct." I took his advice and made the "High Road" lecture into a hot gospel show. He was tickled pink that the technique worked for a nation as well as for a company.

His best scenario was the one that captured the second oil price shock in the mid-seventies. He talked of "the market entering a zone of anxiety where the principle of irresistible temptation would apply". He was so right – the Rotterdam spot traders saw the market tightening and hoicked the price up from $12 to $30 a barrel. Shell never looked back.

Soon after we met, Pierre invited me to spend a week at Harvard Business School lecturing on a scenario course that he and Professor Bruce Scott had devised. I remember the visit not so much for that as the weekend we all spent at Bruce's country retreat. Being winter, it snowed heavily. So Bruce had the bright idea after a jolly dinner that the three of us would tobogganing down a local country lane known for its steepness. With only a torch to guide us in the dark, we gathered speed and the inevitable happened. We missed a curve and hurtled straight into a snowdrift. It was a soft landing, thank heavens! As we dusted ourselves off, I reflected on the fate of the three futurists who should have known better.

Pierre's greatest compliment was to call you remarkable. You felt you had joined a very select band. Well, Pierre, you were the most remarkable one of them all.

Rosemary Nalden

Rosemary demonstrates just how much one person can achieve with talent and focus.

25.1.1998 Picture this. It's a Saturday morning at the ritzy Hyde Park shopping centre in the northern suburbs of Johannesburg. As I descend on the escalator in the main concourse, I see this string orchestra assembling below me. There are 26 players in all, with a vivacious woman bustling around them, adjusting their music stands and helping them to tune their instruments.

Once they're settled, she switches into the role of conductor and they strike up. Excerpts from *Carmen* and other well-known classical pieces follow. If you close your eyes, you could be listening to the National Symphony Orchestra minus the brass and wind – such is the professionalism and flair of this group. Well-heeled shoppers stop in their tracks and applaud after each piece.

In reality, the musicians belong to the Buskaid Soweto String Project, formed in January 1997 in Diepkloof. They range in age from six to eighteen years. The lady conducting the ensemble is Rosemary Nalden, a freelance viola player with a long stack of international recordings behind her. She's a sub-principal violist in the English Baroque Soloists and a regular member of the London Classical Players as well as other orchestras. In other words, she has impeccable credentials.

She originally heard about the difficulties besetting young Sowetan string players on the BBC's *Today* programme. She then enlisted the support of over one hundred of her professional colleagues who took part in a simultaneous "busk" at sixteen main-line railway stations across Britain. In two hours they raised £6 000 for the benefit of the young township musicians. The money went towards instruments, music, general equipment and transport costs.

On leave from her career in the UK, Rosemary drives herself daily into Soweto to teach the youngsters. She employs a highly specialised string teaching method developed by a Hungarian/American pedagogue, Paul Rolland, and expanded by English teacher Sheila Nelson. It stresses independence and initiative in reading skills – in direct contrast to the Suzuki method of aural dependence. The technique was used to great effect to teach deprived children in the Tower Hamlets are in the East End of London.

In Soweto, it has achieved phenomenal results. Rosemary is staggered at the rate at which these young kids absorb the information offered them. She reckons that, on a random basis, more musical talent is concentrated in Soweto than in a renowned suburb like Hampstead in London. They have already performed with our own NSO and under the baton of John Eliot Gardiner, arguably the busiest recording and performing conductor in the world today. Twice they have been invited to play for President Mandela at presidential functions in Pretoria. In September last year the Buskaid String Quartet was chosen to play at a master class given by the violin virtuoso Pinchas Zukerman. The supreme Tokyo String Quartet visited Soweto to coach them during their recent tour of South Africa.

Two of Rosemary's stars are a brother and sister – Samson and Innocentia Diamond. He (thirteen) plays the violin and she (nine) plays the cello. The shack they live in adjoins a shebeen run by their grandmother. Their mother is away during the day at a factory while their father is permanently unemployed. Despite practising in noisy and cramped surroundings, they could become virtuosos one day as long as they persevere. If Rosemary has anything to do with it, they will. Regular attendance, punctuality, discipline and commitment are qualities Rosemary demands of all participants in the project.

Lessons right now are conducted in a tiny church office, but it is hoped that Soweto will have its first purpose-built, independent music centre by mid-1998. Who knows – one day these kids may be playing at the Royal Albert Hall. Then not only Rosemary but all of us will be proud of the fact that Soweto has proved itself as a centre of world-class classical musicianship.

Bonnie Pon

Bonnie and his family set the night sky alight with their science and artistry.

8.3.1998 Family ties count, I'm thinking, as I vainly try to pick up a piece of duck with chopsticks. I'm at a Chinese restaurant in downtown Johannesburg. Around me are the Pon family who are the best pyrotechnicians in South Africa. In layman's terms, they put on fireworks displays like you've never seen before – not surprising since the art of making and letting off fireworks originated in China.

Bonnie Pon, the leader of the pack when it comes to mounting the displays, is sitting next to me. Before we came to the restaurant, he introduced me to his mother, Sui-Chee, who at 84 still runs the supermarket down the road which specialises in provisions from the Far East. She started out in the neighbourhood with a small trading store 53 years ago. Bonnie, together with his three brothers and four sisters, was brought up in a block of flats across the street. It's all a stone's throw away from where I work in 44 Main Street.

The display which made me want to meet the Pons was the one they put on at the annual concert of the National Symphony Orchestra in the grounds of the Johannesburg College of Education. I've never been before and wasn't warned about the awesome spectacle which occurred during the grand finale of Tchaikovsky's 1812 symphony. I'd expected a few cannonlike noises at the most. So while I'm a great fan of the NSO and its director Richard Cock (who is the principal force behind the growing popularity of classical music in South Africa) and they did play some beautiful pieces, the evening from my point of view went to Pon. I think I was at least supported in this judgement by all the children milling around in the crowd of 10 000 that watched the concert.

At the lunch, Bonnie explains to me that, because of the bangs, several members of the orchestra wear earplugs and therefore have to watch the conductor very carefully during the symphony. Nine people – seven of whom are family, one his daughter's boyfriend ("not family yet") and one full-time worker – set up the display in the afternoon. Erwin, Bonnie's son, is a registered pyrotechnician at the same time as studying at Wits. His niece, Jocelyn, finds time to be a key member of the team in her busy schedule of running a travel agency. His wife, Margaret, assists too.

The show consists of 300 shells fired from mortars which leave spherical patterns in the sky measuring between 150 and 200 metres in diameter. These are the stars, so to speak, of the show. As soon as you hear the low bass sound of the mortar, you anticipate the explosive burst of colours overhead. They look as if they'll fall down right on top of you. In addition, there are two giant Catherine wheels, two waterfalls which rain white light, fifty skyrockets with the conventional comet tail and a variety of 64 ground displays.

The Pons have been in the fireworks display business for eight years; but they've been putting on a private show in the neighbourhood parking lot for fifty years to usher in the New Year. Apart from the NSO concert, they've done Independence Day celebrations in Botswana, Namibia and the Seychelles. They do the one-day cricket internationals at the Wanderers where a six gets a shell and fifty runs or a hat-trick of wickets earns a fifteen-second display. They've performed on a rolling ship at sea off Mozambique, indoors at the Extravaganza at Sun City (using special smokeless fireworks from America) and for the Rolling Stones' Voodoo Lounge tour at Ellis Park. Even pelting rain and thunderstorms won't stop them. Once the fountain at the Randburg Waterfront switched on halfway through a display on the island and the Pons weren't fazed.

I asked the family which was the most memorable occasion. They agreed it was a display for just two people, a Russian and his daughter who stood on a balcony at the Palace. It was her 21st birthday. As Bonnie jested, he must have had money to burn!

Agatha Christie

I would give Agatha a medal just for her ability to play croquet and bridge. However, as the premier writer of crime in this century, she qualifies too.

15.3.1998 She placed her ball behind mine, raised her wooden mallet, carefully took aim and whacked the two balls with extreme vigour in the direction of the flowerbed. Mine, being the front one, raced at great speed into the roses while hers remained relatively static and well positioned for the next croquet hoop. "So sorry," she said with a slightly mischievous smile, "but it's all part of the game." With her wispy white hair and bustling manner, she reminded me of Miss Marple. This wasn't surprising since she was the one who created the fictional character in the first place. Agatha Christie was as purposeful about winning at croquet (and bridge at which I subsequently partnered her that evening) as she was at writing her detective novels.

I had the great fortune of spending a few days with her and her archaeologist husband, Sir Max Mallowan, at their summer home near Torquay in Devon. It was a sunny July in 1965, perfect for cucumber sandwiches and China tea on the porch after exerting oneself on the croquet lawn. I knew her grandson pretty well from playing cricket with him at school and university. On his 21st birthday, she gave him all past and future royalties to *The Mousetrap*, the longest running play ever in the history of London's West End – certainly a gift not to be sneezed at! If I'm not mistaken, the play is still on.

Why am I reminiscing like this? Because I'm on holiday and, having raided the bookshelves of my parents-in-law, I am ensconced in *Dead Man's Folly* – one of the 77 novels Agatha wrote. It is another era she tells tales of, when engines were steam and cheats were cads. For example, a delicious excerpt goes like this: "Poirot nodded absently. He was reflecting, not for the first time, that seen from the back, shorts were becoming to very few of the female sex. He shut his eyes in pain. Why, oh why, must young women array themselves thus?" One has a sneaking feeling that

195

these words more accurately reflected the sentiments of Agatha than Hercule. He himself was described as "applying a scented pomade to his moustaches and twirling them to a ferocious couple of points". Later, when temporarily baffled by the crime "his ego was seriously deflated – even his moustaches drooped". Agatha's references to her Belgian detective never lacked for wit.

During my formative years, Bulldog Drummond and Dan Dare, the famous space commander of the *Eagle* comics who fought in the 1950s antecedent to *Star Wars*, vied with Sherlock Holmes and Doctor Watson for my affections. A new dimension was added when I was fifteen. My Classics master introduced me to Homer's *Odyssey*. The bit I remember most was when Odysseus (or Ulysses) was captured by the giant Cyclops, Polyphemus, who immediately devoured six of his colleagues. Odysseus then made Polyphemus drunk with wine, blinded him in his one eye with a burning pole, and escaped with his companions by concealing himself and them under the bellies of the sheep which the Cyclops let out of his cave. Written in ancient Greek rhyme around 850 BC, Homer's *Iliad* and *Odyssey* were probably the first two bloodthirsty, action-packed thrillers to gain international acclaim.

Nowadays, John Grisham and Patricia Cornwall rule the literary roost, he with his legal experience and she with her knowledge of autopsies and morgues. Their themes of good versus evil with good tracking down and triumphing over evil in the end are eternal. People want heroes who catch criminals. On television *Blue Heelers* in Australia, *The Bill* in Britain and *Murder She Wrote* in America have drawn peak audiences at prime time. In the last mentioned series, Angela Lansbury plays Jessica Fletcher, an updated replica of Miss Marple. It's been a favourite in South Africa too. It goes to show that Agatha's legacy lives on everywhere.

Colin Hall

Colin gets a medal for putting his finger on the real limiting factor to an improvement in productivity in South Africa – fear of standing out from the crowd, and fear of being made to look stupid if you do so. World-class companies go out of their way to create an environment conducive to drawing creative ideas out of people.

5.4.1998 "Hands up those who can sing!" said the speaker to a packed auditorium. Of the audience of 450 business people, about six raised their hands – and even then, tentatively, not ostentatiously. "That's surprising," he remarked, "because I was talking to a Grade O class the other day and they all put up their hands, shouting eagerly 'Me, Sir'. But then, I repeated the request to a bunch of ten-year-olds and guess what the response was: 60 per cent, and the thirteen-year-olds: 20 per cent. As you get older, you become more self-conscious. The fear that you're going to make a fool of yourself in front of everybody stifles your natural energy."

Colin Hall, CEO of Wooltru, warmed to his topic. "Yet I visited a centre for handicapped people in Mitchell's Plain recently where they do carpentry. One guy couldn't hold his limbs still but he announced that he could put a small piece of wood through a circular saw. Do you know how difficult that is because of the forces involved? But he did it perfectly, straight as an arrow. Everybody in the place was using their human energy to the full as they made things and crated them. There was a crackle in the air. In contrast, you lot in this auditorium are claiming a disability you do not possess. Of course you can sing!"

By now, the audience were entranced. You could hear a pin drop. "The problem is," Colin continued, "we carry this attitude across to our work. Of the potential human energy in the average South African workforce, only 5 per cent is being utilised. Nevertheless, many companies manage to get by with just the five-percenters. Imagine how the performance of these companies would improve if we multiplied the energy level by a factor of 10 to 20. How do we do this?"

Pausing like a Southern Baptist preacher, Colin allowed the question to sink in before providing the answer. "You have to recognise that fear is the greatest source of negative energy and love the primary source of positive energy. That said, the management style of most South African companies is designed to instil fear. Darwin rules – it's dog eat dog. You either climb on the shoulders of your colleagues or they climb on yours. If you don't win, you lose. If you're not in control, things are out of control. Macho talk, minimum energy."

Stunned that a hard-headed businessman could talk about business in these terms, the audience leaned forward expectantly for the conclusion. Colin was not about to disappoint them. "There's an African word – *Seriti*. It normally means dignity. But the alternative meaning is the shadow individuals cast when they are projecting their true selves. When a sculptor makes a giraffe out of a piece of tree trunk, it's as important that he knows which wood is not going to be the giraffe as that which is. In the same way, we must strip away all the defensive layers that we've added over the years – and we know don't belong to us – in order to get back to our *Seriti*. Then, like those heroes in Mitchell's Plain, we can release our full human energy. It starts from the inside and works outwards."

The kind of spiritual "Full Monty" that Colin is asking for appeals to me. I've seen too many people over the years change for the worse as a result of fear of failure. They deceive others for so long that they end up deceiving themselves. On the other hand, world-class organisations view failure as part of the natural learning curve. You have to go through the dark night of the innovator to succeed in the end. Divisive competition is replaced by a positive environment which encourages everybody to be true to themselves, give 100 per cent and sing!

Manuel De Castro

Walvis Bay has never been the same since Manuel became its mayor. It is an example for any city or town in South Africa to follow.

26.4.1998 Manuel De Castro. With a name like that, you'd think he was the brother of Fidel and a resident of Cuba. While his nickname was Fidel at school, he is actually of Portuguese ancestry and lives in Walvis Bay in Namibia. He's been mayor of the town for the last four years. Everybody says he's the best thing to happen to Walvis Bay since the South Africans left.

Under Manuel's leadership, Walvis Bay is clean and safe (for that matter so is Windhoek). It's as though the 52 000 residents have clubbed together to say: this is our town and we're going to maintain decent standards. Is any South African city "our town"? The CBD of Johannesburg doesn't evoke a sense of belonging in many people and Durban and Cape Town certainly aren't home to the residents of the adjoining townships. Namibia has a lot to teach us about creating a sense of community in an urban environment.

Manuel has played a key role in attracting other businesses to Walvis Bay to complement its traditional industry of fishing, which has the drawback of offering only seasonal employment. An EPZ (export processing zone) has been established next door to the town, where no corporation taxes of any kind are levied and, interestingly, there's a five-year moratorium on strikes. In the middle of the desert, therefore, has sprung up an industrial township mainly consisting of light engineering businesses. It clearly demonstrates the pulling power of EPZs for entrepreneurs intent on maximising their returns out of exports. But to qualify for a site in Walvis Bay's EPZ, only 70 per cent of a company's production has to be exported. The rest can be sold locally in Namibia.

Nevertheless, the real potential for Walvis Bay is as a tourist resort because it offers unique experiences to anyone visiting the place. The trump card is the desert. My wife and I were taken for a short trip into it in a 4 x 4. Jan, our driver, tapped the dashboard for luck as he revved the engine to climb the dunes, and then took us on near-vertical descents where you felt the vehicle had to go front-over-rear to get to the bottom. He showed us the large, round, green fruit of the Narra plant with its spiky skin. The Topnaars, whose numbers are down to 3 000 and who live in the desert, harvest the fruit and extract the pips. These are exported to Germany and added to confectionery as an aphrodisiac – you learn something new every day!

We visited the site of a First World War German camp where you could examine pieces of original crockery and bottles as well as make out the footprints of oxen used to draw sleighs of military equipment across the sand. Even the holes where the officers pitched their tents were still visible. We saw desert graveyards of humans and animals where the bones had lain for decades in tidy white piles. We took pictures of Dune Seven – the granddaddy of them all – where they have annual fireworks displays. We had a drink in a wooden pub at the end of a jetty called "Lang Strand", followed by a spectacular meal of fish in a restaurant close by. The previous evening the proprietors had served braai-ed oysters in the desert to a party of 250 off a cruise ship that had docked in the port. Quite an undertaking! And if that's not enough, the lagoon is a birder's paradise, home to pelicans and flamingos among the more than eighty species to be found in the area.

Manuel is sitting on a treasure trove. Good luck to him and the rest of the inhabitants of Walvis Bay.

Emily Hobhouse

I like people with a cause, who go against the flow. When I was recently looking at photographs of the concentration camps in Bloemfontein's Anglo-Boer War Museum, I was struck by the neatness of the rows of little white tents in the open veld. But then my eye was caught by a picture of a skeletally thin child lying on a makeshift bed inside one of the tents. It was a horrible reminder of what a pitiless, beastly business war is. There is no glory in causing kids to end up that way.

9.8.1998 Bloemfontein is already gearing up to mark the centenary of a war in which the number of women and children who died in concentration camps was more than double the number of men from the two opposing sides killed on the battlefield. We are of course talking of the Anglo-Boer War which started at 5 pm on 11 October 1899 and officially ended at 11 pm on 31 May 1902 with the signing ot the Treaty of Vereeniging. The toll amongst white and black civilians in the concentration camps was estimated at around 28 000 of which 4 000 were women and 22 000 were children. In comparison, the number of Boers killed in action amounted to about 5 000 and British soldiers 7 000, making a total combatant toll of 12 000.

The war was always going to be a fairly one-sided affair as long as the British taxpayer was prepared to stump up the money required to finance it. But patriotism was rife, so there was no problem. The British Election in 1900 was actually called the "Khaki Election". The ruling Conservatives won it with the slogan "a vote for the Liberals is a vote for the Boers" and were thus mandated to finish the war. The number of men the British eventually used in the war was around 550 000 including 100 000 black and coloured personnel who mainly provided logistical support. Against this, the Boers managed to muster 78 000 commandos, including 3 000 foreign volunteers and 15 000 Cape and Natal rebels. Outnumbered seven to one and with fewer weapons, the Boers still gave the British a run for their money. Due to tenacity, local knowledge and guerilla tactics, they managed to prolong "the fight of the kopjes" for a period of more than two and a half years and at a cost to the British tax-payer of £200 million.

The war was roughly divided into two phases. The first consisted of set piece battles and sieges, and ended with the annexation of the Transvaal in September 1900. From then on, it was a mobile war of skirmishes which Kitchener turned into a war of attrition. He adopted a scorched-earth policy of burning Boer farms suspected of providing support to the commandos, erected blockhouses as a means of controlling the countryside and established concentration camps for the noncombatants. His thoroughness, which might have been justified from a military point of view, exacted a terrible price in innocent lives. Milner called the tragedy of the concentration camps "a sad fiasco". Dishonest contractors, inefficient officials, ill-chosen sites for the camps and epidemics of measles and pneumonia which broke out in May 1901 raised the death toll amongst inmates to 344 per thousand.

The only British person of note to emerge from the war with

an enhanced reputation was Emily Hobhouse, a social worker who was born near Liskeard in Cornwall in 1860 and spent the first thirty-five years of her life leading a sheltered existence at her father's rectory. However, on learning of the high mortality rate in the concentration camps in South Africa, she took up the cudgels on behalf of the Boers. She founded the South African Women and Children's Distress Fund, and spent five months in the camps doing her best to alleviate the suffering.

On her return to Britain, she caused a political sensation with her report condemning conditions in the camps. It prompted the leader of the Liberal opposition, Sir Henry Campbell-Bannerman, to state that the campaign against the Boers used "methods of barbarism". To grateful Boer women, Hobhouse became known as the "Angel of Love". After the war was over, she returned to the Orange Free State in 1903 to assist in the education of women and girls. She died in London in 1926, but her ashes are interred at the foot of the Women's Memorial in Bloemfontein.

John Harrison

Anybody who discovered how to measure longitude accurately deserves a medal for all the lives he has subsequently saved at sea.

3.5.1998 A few minutes after taking off on a recent flight across the Pacific, the pilot informed us that, given the weather conditions en route, we would be touching down about ten minutes behind schedule. Eight hours later, he was proved correct within a matter of seconds.

Less than three hundred years ago, such a calculation would have been unthinkable even if Leonardo da Vinci's dream of manned flight had been possible. This becomes obvious from reading *Longitude* by Dava Sobel, "the true story of a lone genius who solved the greatest scientific problem of his time".

The genius was John Harrison, British clockmaker extraordinary, whose life spanned exactly 83 years from 24 March 1693 to 24 March 1776.

Before he turned his mind to maritime timekeeping, accidents at sea due to miscalculations of longitude were frequent. It was fairly easy for sailors to estimate latitude from the length of the day, or by the height of the sun or well-known stars above the horizon. In contrast, to learn one's longitude at sea, one needed to know the local time aboard ship and also the time at the home port at that very same moment. Since the Earth takes 24 hours to complete a full revolution of 360°, one hour represents 15°. Hence each hour's time difference between the ship and the starting point marks a progress to the east or west of 15°. Depending on the ship's latitude, an arc of 15° corresponds to a different distance travelled – 68 miles at the equator, virtually zero at the poles.

Without two accurate watches – one reflecting time in the home port and the other reset each day to local noon when the sun reaches its highest point in the sky – ships' captains had to rely on "dead reckoning". This was a combination of instinct and an assortment of exceptionally crude measures of speed and direction of travel. As Sobel observes, dead reckoning too often led to dead men. The most famous example of error took place on the foggy night of 22 October 1707 when 2 000 men died on the rocks of the Scilly Isles. Of the two who swam to shore and survived, Admiral Sir Clowdisley Shovell, the leader of the fleet, was one. He was promptly murdered on the beach by a local woman who wanted the emerald ring on his finger. Three decades later, she confessed to the crime on her deathbed. Shovell's fate was regarded as just deserts by some: a few hours earlier he'd hanged a seaman who was brave enough to disagree with him about the fleet's location for mutiny.

The tragedy, however, was one in a chain of events which resulted in the Longitude Act passed by the English Parliament in 1714. It offered a king's ransom of £20 000 for anyone whose method or device solved the problem of longitude. A race for the prize developed between astronomers on the one hand and a lone clockmaker – Harrison – on the other. Between 1730 and 1759, Harrison constructed four clocks, one of which took him nineteen years to complete. Each design yielded greater accuracy, overcoming the problems of pitching and rolling decks and changing temperatures. The Machiavellian nature of the Board of Longitude, established to bestow the prize, meant that Harrison only grudgingly and belatedly was given proper compensation in 1773. It required the intervention of George III for the final instalment to be paid. Even then he wasn't acknowledged as the prizewinner. Thank heavens he lived long enough to get what he did.

"The Harrisons" (as the four clocks have become known) now reside appropriately at Greenwich, site of the prime meridian, zero longitude. H-1, H-2 and H-3 tick away but the hands of H-4 which looks more like a pocket watch than a sea clock are frozen. It's too valuable to wind up. Sobel's final words sum it all up beautifully: "He wrested the world's whereabouts from the stars, and locked the secret in a pocket watch."

Moira Lovell
Her slim books of poetry contain many powerful thoughts.

17.5.1998

> *A thing of beauty is a joy for ever:*
> *Its loveliness increases; it will never*
> *Pass into nothingness; but still will keep*
> *A bower quiet for us, and a sleep*
> *Full of sweet dreams, and health, and quiet breathing*

I will carry the opening lines of Keats' "Endymion" to my grave. I was made to learn it at school. It's probably the reason why I don't read as much poetry as I should. Imagine having the talent to write words like "Thou still unravished bride of quietness. Thou foster-child of silence and slow time" to portray a figure on a Grecian urn. Only a poet can do that and die tragically of TB at the age of 25. But the pen is mightier than disease as well as the sword. The verses of Keats will live on forever.

A slim volume of poetry that was thrust into my hands the other day caused me to reminisce thus. It's called *Departures* by Moira

Lovell. She lives close to Pietermaritzburg and she writes with the same electricity as Keats. Obviously, her style is more modern. How's this for describing a Christmas dinner in South Africa:

> *Rolls of razor-gut crown the garden wall;*
> *The bellies of crackers are arsenals;*
> *Uneasy as kings in our paper crowns,*
> *We hear the carolling of the sirens*
> *While gifts, less lasting than gold, we proffer,*
> *Less holy than incense, less healing than myrrh.*

Lovell in another poem describes how she saves a locust from the swimming pool:

> *I net the locust*
> *And toss it onto the warm stones*
> *Where it squats stupidly*
> *Wet through under the sun*
> *Neglecting to thank me.*

Later on, in the poem, Lovell likens humans to locusts when it comes to ingratitude for lucky escapes:

> *The long rod that must reach out of the sky*
> *And scoop someone up*
> *In its net*
> *To sit stupidly*
> *Stunned in the sun*
> *Neglecting to say thank you.*

Elsewhere in the book Lovell writes on our materialistic tendencies these days:

> *Nowadays,*
> *Self-styled Noahs abound,*
> *Building arks.*
> *Telephones,*

Two; two televisions;
Vehicles, two.

The great thing about good poetry is that you grab a thought out of the air with a few words. Lovell's final sonnet is on death itself:

Accustomed to the stretch of working days
That seemed to be all labour, little love;
Accustomed to the shrinking time to play
Or scribble little pieces for one's oeuvre.
Yet leaving will be harder than in youth
When mystery and promise hid the truth.

These are lines for the younger generation to consider. Maybe we should work less and play a little more in our brief span on Earth. Certainly we should watch less television and read more poetry.

St Mary's Waverley
Another school that deserves a medal for the originality of demon-strating to parents the wonders of science.

14.6.1998 I've always believed that humour is a good way to sell serious ideas. A funny story will always stick in people's minds and then they remember the idea associated with it.

I came across the use of the technique in an unlikely setting – the science laboratory at St Mary's Waverley in Johannesburg. This outstanding school for girls celebrated its 110th anniversary by having an open day a few weekends ago. I wandered around the lab marvelling at the practical experiments done by the girls to show their parents the wonders of the physical world. In one corner electrons raced through a cathode ray tube leaving an eerie pink glow, while in another iron filings magically aligned themselves to the forces of an invisible magnetic field. One girl asked me to pull apart two hemispheres from which the air had been emptied. I was unable to do so – thank heavens no-one else could either! This signified the mighty presence of atmospheric pressure. Then she pumped air in again – whereupon the two halves just fell apart.

But what really caught my eye was a series of written anecdotes about the great men behind the experiments being demonstrated. Did you know that James Joule, after whom the unit of energy is named, was an English brewer for whom science was a hobby? He spent his honeymoon running up and down a waterfall in Switzerland measuring the temperature difference of the water at the bottom compared to the top (it is warmer at the bottom). His unimpressed bride observed these antics whilst perched on a rock.

André Ampère, a Frenchman who gave his name to electric current, used to blow his nose on the blackboard duster during lectures and once solved an equation by writing it out on the roof of a cab. When Napoleon Bonaparte visited the Paris Academy, Ampère didn't recognise him. Subsequently Ampère was invited to dine at the palace, but forgot about the invitation and didn't turn up.

Alessandro Volta, an Italian, submitted a manuscript in March 1800 to the Royal Society in England describing the invention of the voltaic pile, which was the forerunner to the battery. The two men in charge of publications at the Society shelved Volta's manuscript and published his discovery under their own names. Fortunately they were exposed as scientific plagiarists and vanished. Volta was rightly credited with the invention, which is why we measure potential difference in volts.

Michael Faraday, the experimental genius of the nineteenth century, was the son of a blacksmith and had little formal education. He was apprenticed to a bookbinder but soon changed direction because of his scientific curiosity. If he had lived today he would have won at least six Nobel prizes for his discoveries. He was offered a knighthood but declined it on the grounds that he wanted to be known as plain Mr Faraday.

The last story I came across concerns one of the all-time great scientists, Isaac Newton. Incidentally, he was born in the same year that Galileo died – 1642. He made a hole in his door so that his cat could move in and out of the house freely. When the cat had kittens, he added a number of small holes to the big one. Ah, even scientists have foibles!

Big Guy

You may think it odd that I award an animal a medal, but Big Guy is as important for the future of tourism in this country as any other factor. At speed, he was very special.

1.11.1998 Big Guy is giving me the beady eye. He doesn't appear to be short-sighted like the books say he is. Maybe his senses of smell and hearing which are supposed to be keener than his sight have located me on his radar screen. He certainly knows I'm there!

I'm sitting in the front of an open Land Rover in the Welgevonden Game Reserve, north-west of Vaalwater in the Northern Province. The rest of the party, perched on tiered benches behind me, are similarly apprehensive. Petrus, the driver alongside me, idles the engine. Big Guy, a three-ton, square-mouthed rhinoceros, twitches his ears, snorts and goes back to chewing the grass.

Then he starts to move. Not directly towards us, but definitely closer to the dirt road we're on. He's uneasy. We're uneasy. I start remembering all those tales when it was in vogue to shoot anything that moved in the bush including these awesome creatures. Sometimes the rhino charged through a hail of bullets and managed to trample the hunter to death.

Now, thank heavens, we carry cameras, not rifles. And he's an endangered species. Only poachers seek to perforate his legendary thick skin for the horn that is supposedly an aphrodisiac. Maybe Viagra will destroy the market. How's this for a slogan: "Save the rhino, take a Viagra!"

But back to Big Guy. He's now on the road a few yards in front of our bonnet pointing in the same direction as us. His big behind, stumpy legs and saggy, baggy skin are overwhelming.

The view is solid grey. From the back, he resembles a gargantuan version of my Staffordshire bull terrier.

Then he begins trotting away from us down the road. Nothing clumsy. It's an agile movement with all four legs in perfect synchronicity. Petrus engages first gear and we follow. I wonder how fast Big Guy can wheel around and face us, were it to take his fancy. It also crosses my mind that a Land Rover isn't that fast in reverse. I look for possible escape routes into the bush but how can you hide a Land Rover behind a thorn tree? Petrus on the other hand looks unconcerned.

Suddenly Big Guy switches gear, from a lolloping stride into a flat-out gallop. Judging from the Land Rover's speed and the fact that he is disappearing down the road in front of us, I guess he must be doing around 40 kilometres an hour. All that bone, muscle and flesh going at that speed – is there a natural steroid in the grass? I pray and hope that a vehicle is not coming in the other direction because they're going to get an awful surprise to meet Big Guy rounding the corner at full tilt.

Luckily, no-one materialises and all we see ahead of us is a cloud of dust in the road, a golden haze in the sun's rays. Obviously sprinting is good for his bowel movements as we swerve to avoid a steaming heap the size of Kilimanjaro located on one of the bends. Maybe he's marking out his territory. Then we see him again, standing in the road looking back at us. He's covered two kilometres at maximum velocity. No sweat, no panting after breaking all human records over the distance. Then he turns and sidles off into the bush.

He's gone. We're off his radar screen. I cross myself off the list of endangered species, meanwhile reflecting that one in nine jobs in the world is associated with tourism. It's the biggest industry there is, employing 250 million people. Its proportion of global GDP is 8 per cent. South Africa's figure is 4 per cent. Crazy when we have Big Guy as our competitive advantage.

Sandi Krige and Edward De Bono

I reckon Sandi has come up with the slogan that should take us into the next millennium. De Bono gets a medal for putting her in the right frame of mind.

18.10.1998 "I work for Africa: Africa works for me." While I would love to lay claim to this slogan, I have to state that the honour goes to Sandi Krige. She, along with a number of other business people including myself, was attending a dinner in Johannesburg in honour of Dr Edward De Bono. After he spoke, each of the seven tables present was asked to come up with three suggestions which would facilitate the African renaissance.

Sandi, a marketing executive, did some lateral thinking along De Bono lines and came up with this brilliant caption. What I like about the phrase is the symbiotic relationship inherent in it. Only if you work for Africa will Africa work for you. More broadly, only if you feel the obligation to do something for the community do you have the right to receive anything from it. Thus, Sandi's brainwave neatly combines the spirit of Ubuntu with the importance of individual effort.

How did De Bono motivate Sandi to come up with such an innovative theme? He began by pointing out that the structure of Western thinking is to this day heavily dependent upon the teachings of the "gang of three" – Socrates, Plato and Aristotle. Socrates taught us to argue; Plato programmed us to seek eternal truths; and Aristotle told us to apply logic in getting there.

The net result of the input from these three is that when we debate important issues in groups, we tend to follow courtroom procedure. First an idea is proposed; then arguments are led for and against the idea; then the logic of these arguments is weighed up; and then we decide on the truth or falsity of the idea. Because the group is thinking in many dimensions at the same time, members are often at odds with each other where no genuine differences exist. Above all, we tend to focus on getting to the bottom of what *is* the case rather than imagining what *can be* the case. The process is therefore highly inefficient when it comes to creative thought.

De Bono recommends an approach which lessens group conflict and compels the group to focus on issues in parallel and one at a time. Think of how an architect designs a house with a client. The former is trying to tease out what the latter wants brick by brick, room by room, until the whole house can be visualised. They work in co-operation with one another and settle disagreements as they arise.

This analogy leads De Bono to propose his famous six-hat technique. In any discussion, we should put on one hat at a time exclusively. The first one is the white hat where in a neutral manner we gather all the information relevant to the topic. Then we don the red hat which represents warmth. It permits us to display our feelings, emotions and intuition. This is replaced by a black hat where we move into a phase of caution, risk assessment and criticism. De Bono warns of our tendency to overuse this hat and discount really original thoughts.

The fourth hat is yellow which signifies it's time to be "logical positive" and explore the benefits and values of the idea. Next comes the green hat when we look at alternatives which might be more creative than the idea under review. The last hat is the blue one, at which stage we widen our perspective to see how everything fits into place and to obtain an overview – like the conductor of an orchestra.

Try it out. It worked for Sandi!

Charles Dickens
I give the nod to Dickens on the basis of this charming Christmas story which is so pertinent for the more privileged members of our own society. There's no humbug in helping the poor.

21.12.1997 I have just re-read *A Christmas Carol* by Charles Dickens. A lot of people think it is a book meant for children. It is just as relevant for adults as well.

To remind you of the story, Ebenezer Scrooge is a successful but stingy businessman prone to saying "humbug" about anything that smacks of generosity and goodness – especially Christmas. As he says: "If I could work my will, every idiot who goes about with 'Merry Christmas' on his lips, should be boiled with his own pudding, and buried with a stake of holly through his heart." As for the poor: "If they would rather die, they had better do it, and decrease the surplus population."

He arrives home on Christmas Eve to see the ghostly face of his long-dead partner, Jacob Marley, on the knocker of his front door. Inside, he is greeted by the selfsame ghost "in his pigtail, usual waistcoat, tights, and boots". Around Marley is a long chain "made of cash-boxes, keys, padlocks, ledgers, deeds, and heavy purses wrought in steel". He explains that the spirit of every man walks abroad and "if that spirit goes not forth in life, it is condemned to do so after death. It is doomed to wander through the world – oh, woe is me! – and witness what it cannot share, but might have shared on earth, and turned to happiness." As for being fettered, Marley explains: "I wear the chain I forged in life. I made it link by link, and yard by yard; I girded it on of my free will."

Marley warns Scrooge that on the coming night he will be haunted by three Spirits – the Ghosts of Christmas, Past, Present and Yet to Come. The first Spirit makes Scrooge relive his childhood and in particular the painful split with the young woman he loved. Her parting words are: "Another idol displaced me. I have seen your nobler aspirations fall off one by one, until the master-passion, Gain, engrosses you."

The second Spirit whisks Scrooge to a variety of destinations, demonstrating how at Christmas time people make the most of the occasion, even in the extremest of circumstances. To a lonely hut upon a bleak and deserted moor where a mining family is celebrating, to a lighthouse, to a ship at sea, Scrooge accompanies the Spirit. At one point in the journey, he gazes upon the good cheer of the family of Bob Cratchit, the clerk that he employs for a pittance. He asks after the future of Tiny Tim, the frailest member of the family, who walks on crutches. The Spirit replies: "I see a vacant seat in the poor chimney corner, and a crutch without an owner, carefully preserved. If these shadows remain unaltered by the Future, the child will die."

The last Spirit takes Scrooge to listen in on the future conversation of a group of men with whom "he had made a point always of standing well in their esteem; in a business point of view, that is". "How are you?" asked one. "How are you?" returned the other. "Well," said the first, "old Scratch has got his own at last, hey?" "So I am told," returned the second, "cold, isn't it?" To his horror, Scrooge later learns that this trivial aside to the death of Scratch is actually about him. He asks the Spirit: "Are these the shadows of the things that Will be, or are they the shadows of things that May be, only?"

Luckily, for Scrooge, the future is indeed changeable. He wakes, in the real world, to the sight of his own bedpost on Christmas morning. He immediately sets about repairing the past. He buys a prize turkey for the Cratchit family, raises Bob's salary and vows to look after Tiny Tim "who did NOT die". Scrooge turns into "as good a friend, as good a master, and as good a man, as the good old city knew".

Dickens ends the book on a cheerful note about Scrooge: "It was always said of him, that he knew how to keep Christmas well. May that be truly said of us, and all of us! And so, as Tiny Tim observes, God bless Us, Every One!"

Susan Allison

She gets a medal for her letter to The Star. *Consumer pressure has indeed made several of the South African retail chains drop the sale of magazines that may be offensive to the public.*

5.2.1995 In our Latin class at school, we could not wait to leave the boring historical prose of Caesar and Livy behind for the passionate verse of Catullus and Horace. For pubescent, albeit classical, scholars it was no contest between Caesar's dry comment that "Gallia est omnis divisa in partes tres" (The whole of Gaul is divided into three parts) and the red-blooded observation by Catullus "Sed mulier cupido quod dicit amanti, in vento et rapida scribere oportet aqua" (But what a woman says to her lusting lover it is best to write in wind and swift-flowing water) or his plea "Da mi basia mille, deinde centum, dein mille altera" (Give me a thousand kisses, then a hundred, then a thousand more).

What triggered this memory was a recent letter to *The Star* from Susan Allison of Linden, Johannesburg which began: "Every country that has fallen has fallen from within. History shows that every civilisation that has fallen has been one with an increasing decline in morality. Whether one believes in God or not, from the Roman Empire to the United States, where people disregard moral standards and religious principles there can only be a breakdown in everything – government, marriages, family life, education, etc."

The specific purpose of her letter was to complain about all the girlie magazines now displayed in stores at the eyelevel of her five-year-old daughter. As she says: "I try to avert her eyes, but I see other children looking at these and my heart breaks." This is strong and very sincere stuff, and represents the beginning of a backlash against the burgeoning "soft porn" industry in South Africa. The only surprise is that it has not happened sooner.

"Soft porn" has already developed into a booming industry overseas. The reasons that South Africa has not participated so far have been its political isolation and the Calvinistic beliefs of its previous rulers. For example, virtually every newsagent in London carries a stock of these magazines but – and this goes some way towards solving Susan Allison's problem – they are stacked in a row well above the eyelevel of children. Paul Raymond, owner of Raymond's Revue Bar in Soho and publisher of popular erotica, is reputed to be one of Britain's richest men. The plain fact is that sex sells. It always has done and it always will.

Where there has been a change is in presentation. Modern technology has made sex far more explicit than the innuendoes of the later Roman poets I studied. No attempt is made any longer at subtlety or illusion. Ankles are no longer fleetingly glimpsed. Thanks to the best shutters and lenses available to professional photographers today, everything is permanently on display in the finest and most intimate detail. No double entendre. No beautiful and sensual prose intertwining the theme of love and sex as in

Lady Chatterley's Lover. It's all about flesh and sexual prowess. But that's what the market wants.

Moreover, the still photograph is rapidly yielding in popularity to the moving images of videos and electronic "cyber-sex" offered in personal computer programmes and networks. This is usually not only "hard core" but much more difficult for parents to control and the authorities to detect.

No doubt a large proportion of the South African public are deeply disturbed by what is going on. They are broad-minded, yet find such blatant and crude exploitation of sex thoroughly offensive. They don't like having their freedom transgressed by having to look at provocative magazine covers wherever they shop. They do think there is a direct correlation between pornography and sexual abuse because the status of women is degraded. They also believe that many of the ills of society today can be ascribed to the elevation of sex and the body above love and the soul. They draw a very firm line between freedom and permissiveness. Their judgement is that it is now being crossed.

Then, like Susan Allison, they must speak up. You can be sure that retailers will rapidly adjust the displays on their shelves if they feel they are in danger of losing their solid middle-class customer base. South Africa will be a better place too.

Gray and Becker
Each of them deserves a medal for pointing out the differences between the male and female species.

25.10.1998 Firstly, I read John Gray's *Men are from Mars, Women are from Venus*, which suggested that women possess different neural networks to men. The book offered a practical guide for improving communication and getting what you want in your relationships. Martians (men) value power, competency, efficiency and achievement. They are more interested in results and objects than people and feelings. Venetians (women) value love, communication, beauty and relationships. They want to share their feelings and hear the details (whereas two men can fish together in silence and still feel a mutual bonding).

Chapter three of the book is entitled "Men Go to Their Caves and Women Talk". While a man under stress tends to focus on one problem and forget all others, a woman under stress tends to expand and become overwhelmed by all her problems. He withdraws into the cave of his mind and becomes unsociable because he wants to solve the problem himself: she finds relief in talking in great detail to someone about every single problem until she has a greater awareness of what is really bothering her. Gray advises both sexes to respect and accept these differences if they want to have lasting and loving relationships with one another.

Secondly, I went to the Alhambra Theatre and watched Rob Becker's comedy *Defending the Caveman* which is more or less on the same theme with some hilarious twists. The play has had a record-breaking run with full houses every night. Tim Plewman is brilliant as a one-man show. Becker's thesis is that we must look at our prehistoric ancestors to trace the origin of our differences. Man went out as a hunter with a spear which demanded focus on a single object – the animal being stalked for the pot – which once dispatched allowed him to shift to the next object. He was sequential in his approach – kill and then move on. Woman went out as a gatherer of anything of value which was to hand. Thus she developed all-round vision while searching for fruits, seeds and fuel (and at the same time looking after the kids). Whereas a man, the loner, naturally negotiates in any group situation to optimise his own individual position, a woman naturally co-operates with the rest of the group to optimise the collective result. Man is driven by the zero-sum outlook of "I win only if you lose." Woman wants win-win because otherwise it will be lose-lose.

Gray buttresses his argument by saying that when a man is in the cave (like when he's watching television), he will only listen to a woman with 5 per cent of his mind. He thinks that he is listening but she really desires his full and undivided attention. He wants space, she wants proximity.

Becker produces the example that when a man loses his way in the car, he is far less likely than a woman to pull over and ask a stranger for directions. Instead, he will switch off the radio/tape deck so that he can focus solely on finding the right road himself. He is certainly not going to get out of his mobile cave and reveal his incompetence to another caveman. Anyway, a woman has much less chance of getting lost because she has evolved the ability to do several things at once (like notice the crucial off-ramp at the same time as she is driving down the motorway and conversing with her companions in the car).

Both Gray and Becker hail from California. Their respective wives from whom they learnt so much are Bonnie and Erin. Their works represent a welcome and entertaining reminder that the unisex brigade have gone too far in painting a picture of male and female sameness. Obviously, we all have the same rights and we should have the same opportunities to get on in life. But life would be very dull without behavioural contrasts between the sexes. So, as the French say, *vive la difference!*

Denis Beckett
I'm giving an award to Denis for just being a great South African.

12.7.1998 He's as individualistic as the chairs surrounding his dining-room table. Each one has its own shape, history and capacity to carry weight. I met him first in early 1987 when he was running his own journal, *Frontline*. He was sitting at the back of the audience at the South African Institute of International Affairs situated on Wits University campus.

You couldn't miss him with his height, leather jacket and rather unkempt black hair. He could have been a member of the Jets in *West Side Story*. The occasion was one of my lectures during the six-month roadshow which introduced the possibility of a "High Road" for South Africa. Immediately after the lecture was over, he came up to me and asked whether he could write a critique in his magazine. I said the material was still under wraps until the publication of my book a couple of months later,

217

but I would make sure that his was the first story. He kept to his word, I kept to mine. His name was Denis Beckett.

Yet it was a comment Denis made at the time that stuck in my mind. He was wary of any negotiations leading to a power-sharing relationship between whites and blacks. Nothing less than a colour-blind, one man-one vote, full-blooded democracy would do. This was radical stuff for 1987. In the end, however, he's turned out to be absolutely correct. The power-sharing arrangements have all but dissolved and the ANC are firmly in control as the majority party.

I've met Denis off and on over the years since then. There was a restaurant he particularly liked in Doornfontein which served the best bangers and mash in town. *Frontline* ceased publication and he worked for a time at *The Star* and then at *702* hosting an evening radio show. Always original, always thought provoking. But the next piece that left an indelible impression on me was written in Anglo's flagship magazine *Optima*. It was on the state of township education.

To write a factual account, Denis went and sat at a desk in a maths class and observed the pupils around him. The young guy sitting next to him wrote down "thwem". Denis looked at the blackboard and realised that the teacher had slightly miswritten "theorem". The student had painstakingly reproduced a perfect copy of the error in his notebook. As Denis said in his article, the terrible thing wasn't that the student had no concept. It was that he had no concept that he had no concept. With acute observation and one sentence, Denis demolished the century-old ritual of rote-learning which had herded many unfortunate students through their grades with zero learning and understanding. Is it any better today?

Of course, Denis subsequently became a famous television presenter. *Beckett's Trek* was required viewing as Denis examined every nook and cranny of our society and exposed our foibles. Nevertheless, the episode that most fascinated me was when he went into an Aboriginal suburb in Sydney, Australia. At first, the locals thought the film crew was Australian and reacted with extreme hostility. When the penny dropped that they were South

African, the attitude changed in a flash to one of delight that they were being afforded the opportunity to reveal the cracks in Oz.

Denis has written two books on the series – *Trekking* and *Madibaland*. It's the second one which I find more appealing because, in his inimitable way, he reiterates the colour-blind vision that he first proclaimed to me in 1987. He looks forward to "one nation, free and open and actually tolerant, respecting the application of skills more than the complexion of the holders, recognising individuals rather than a race or gender rank order of South Africanness, judging not by the colour of the skin but the content of the character".

When South Africa settles down and the sheer competitiveness of international markets make merit the only feasible criterion for selection, Denis will once again be proved right. Then the rainbow nation will be genuine.

Guild Cottage
Guild Cottage is a gem of an NGO working in one of the most harrowing fields – treating troubled and abused children. It has just celebrated its 91st anniversary. Zelda Kruger as Director of the centre should receive special mention.

8.11.1998 Child abuse is a real problem in South Africa. Here is a story as told in its own words by Guild Cottage, a special home for abused kids in Johannesburg.

"'Another incest victim', said the Child Welfare Worker, requesting a place for a new little girl, in our residential programme. She was called Sue. Aged 8. History – violent alcoholic father, jailed for the abuse of his only daughter. Mother – battered wife, unaware of the abuse, which had started when Sue was only . . . 4 years old. At our first meeting with Sue and her mother, they did not speak to one another. Sue sat, numbly, staring into space. Her mother cried and raged. Yet they desperately needed help. The abuse was traumatic for both of them.

"Families coming to Guild Cottage need to want to be helped, before we can accept them for treatment. Sue was accepted into care for the normal period of one year. At the same time we offered treatment and counselling to her mother.

"At first, Sue was bossy, a mini adult, who avoided bathing and had bad nightmares. Play therapy began immediately. In the daily programme the professional treatment team began to tackle the bathing issue, because Sue had problems with touching her body. A very real problem with abused children. We talked about the abuse – and her feelings. She did not really understand what had happened to her, she viewed it as 'weird, rude and unnatural'. Then we read with her *Mary-Jo's Story*, a Guild Cottage Publication. A short story about an incest victim, just like herself. That proved to be the breakthrough. In her next play session she drew a washing line with clothes on it – her clothes, all her own 'dirty linen' had been washed. At last Sue felt she was not alone, she wasn't so different, and she wasn't so bad, after all.

"By drawing and talking, we tackled her nightmares so she could come to terms with her feelings, and we encouraged her to be a child again. Doing things that all little girls like, such as playing house-house and school-school. Sue's mother was helped by a counsellor to explore the painful problems of her own childhood, and understand how those problems had led to Sue's sexual abuse. We gave her our publication, *The A – Z of Child Sexual Abuse*. Like so many adults, she was amazed how little she had known or understood.

"Sue stayed at Guild Cottage during the week, growing in understanding and self-confidence. Weekends and holidays were spent with her mother developing and strengthening their relationship. Last month Sue went home. Hand in hand with her mother. A laughing child with a new found joy for life. And we will keep in touch, for as long as we are needed."

A. P. Jones

I am awarding this shop a medal because it is the only place I can purchase "empire builders" in South Africa.

29.3.1998 My normal morning "constitutional" takes me around the perimeter of Johannesburg Zoo. Despite the high fences imprisoning humans and animals alike on either side of the road, the trees make the route interesting. I'm usually togged out in a Woollies T-shirt, size fifteen trainers (hard to find) and "empire builders" from A.P. Jones in Fish Hoek – long shorts popular among pukka Englishmen when Victoria was Queen. At my age, a constitutional involves walking the uphills, jogging the downhills and having an open mind about the flat sections depending on how strong I feel.

On this particular Sunday, I decided to add in an extra leg by going around Zoo Lake on the other side of Jan Smuts Avenue. There, as I was surveying a couple of scruffy ducks rootling through somebody's ex-picnic from the day before, I met a Johannesburg advocate for whom I have a great deal of respect and affection. He was striding the other way. We stopped and after exchanging hellos I muttered that I was vainly trying to reduce my girth, tapping the mild convexity of my stomach at the same time (it doesn't qualify yet as a *boep*). He did the same to his. And it suddenly occurred to me that the current global obsession with being lean and trim had raked in two extra victims. We didn't even talk about the weather.

A couple of days previously, I had read a newspaper article on how it's harder to slim the older you get. Scientists say that those who eat moderately and exercise regularly all their lives are still prone to middle-age spread. This applies especially to the male waist and female rear. An average man gains about 7,3 kg and about 120 cm round the waist for each decade of life regardless of whether he runs less than 10 km or more than 40 km a week. People simply need fewer calories as they age because of hormonal changes, reduced metabolism and the decline in muscle bulk, which is one of the major determinants of the amount of energy spent.

Such a formula would suggest a redefinition of obesity. Quite a few health experts and weight tables published in popular magazines suggest that if you put on *any* weight after leaving school, that's bad. You're a glutinous blimp. For women, a feeling of false guilt is intensified by photographs of skeletally thin models without any rider that such a shape is virtually impossible to retain after a certain age. Gaunt is good. Indeed, these photographs positively promote anorexia among those young girls who are not naturally skinny and can only attain that condition through starving themselves.

My interpretation of the results of the American study is that, in advancing age, you can be quite healthy without having to have a svelte figure. Moreover, the ideal pushed by inventors of miracle diet programmes and drugs, peddlers of exercise equipment, owners of health clubs and sweat merchants generally that we should all look like marathon runners is plainly ridiculous and introduces needless stress into our lives.

It's a late twentieth-century myth that instead of doing less as we get older, we should do more. Of course, we have to remain fit. But consistent moderation in everything and a gracious acceptance of the ageing process are better watchwords for longevity than mindless, repetitive exercise. Ask all the "wrinklies" who take the occasional early morning dip on Fish Hoek beach. They know.

Tulbagh
It's fitting to close the awards ceremony with a medal for the plucky residents of Tulbagh.

7.6.1998 The terrible earthquake in Afghanistan brings to mind one that happened nearly thirty years ago here in South Africa. An article in the *Cape Times*, Wednesday, 1 October 1969 read as follows: "The once thriving little Boland centre of Tulbagh looked like a ghost town yesterday. Its business doors closed to hide ruined merchandise, its homes without people, the town lay in the hot September sun, and seemingly tried to catch its breath. But the breath that was once Tulbagh will never return."

The earthquake occurred at 22:05 on the Monday night. We know that because several pendulum clocks in the town stopped then (one of which is in the museum). An eyewitness account described how the quietness of the night was shattered by tremendous explosive sounds followed by a gigantic roaring, rumbling noise rolling forward like waves of a stormy sea. Stupefied people rushed outside over broken glass and fallen plaster.

The surrounding mountains resembled a city of lights as falling rocks acted like flints on the tinder-dry vegetation and started fires. Many thought that the end of the world had come. Some in their terror fled in their cars, while others gathered in groups in open spaces, and waited, shivering, for the morning. A few risked entering their crumbling houses to look for torches, blankets or something to drink. Some brave people offered help at the home of the aged. Measuring 6,4 on the Richter scale, the earthquake killed eleven people. The survivors lived in tents, caravans and prefabricated houses for a long time afterwards. They recall how harsh it was during the subsequent winter nights.

But the breath did return to Tulbagh as my wife and I witnessed on a recent visit to this beautiful farming village. I'll forgive the journalist who wrote the pessimistic piece in the immediate aftermath of the disaster because it's such good prose! He or she simply underestimated the incredible spirit of the residents who turned adversity to advantage. The earthquake put Tulbagh on the map as an historical attraction. The houses in Church Street were lovingly restored to their original architectural designs dating from the eighteenth and nineteenth centuries. The street is now a showpiece of distinctive character and a joy to walk down.

While the Paddagang restaurant is the biggest drawcard for tourists, we decided to have a light meal at Oude Kerk Kombuis on the opposite side of the road. A charming young waitress called M.C. Maritz served me Trophy Honeybush Tea which is alleged to have anti-inflammatory, antiviral and antidepressant properties. Bread is baked in a traditional way in an outside oven and jams include roseleaf, wild cucumber and prickly pear. Unusual fare to say the least! Afterwards, we strolled to a museum which houses a photographic exhibition of the 1969 earthquake. It brought home the extent of the tragedy. Cracked walls and rubble were everywhere. Around 70 per cent of the buildings were destroyed.

Before leaving the area, we drove out of the village into the lee of the mountain chain which bends like a horseshoe around it. Surveying the peaceful valley, I found it hard to imagine the terror people went through. We all talk of "renaissance" now. Tulbagh's been through it.